The River Nene

A guide for river users

Northampton to Peterborough (Dog-in-a-Doublet Lock)
including the Grand Union Canal
(Northampton Arm to Gayton Junction)

IAIN SMITH

Imray Laurie Norie & Wilson

Published by
Imray, Laurie, Norie & Wilson Ltd
Wych House, St Ives,
Cambridgeshire PE27 5BT, England
☎ (01480) 462114
Fax (01480) 496109
2006

Mapping reproduced by permission of
Ordnance Survey on behalf of The
Controller of Her Majesty's Stationery
Office © Crown Copyright

British Library Cataloguing in
Publication Data
A catalogue record for this book is available
from the British Library.

ISBN 978 0 85288 944 2

CAUTION
Every effort has been taken to ensure the
accuracy of this book. It contains selected
information and thus is not definitive and
does not include all known information on
the subject in hand; this is particularly
relevant to the plans which should not be
used for navigation. The author and
publisher believe that its selection is a useful
aid to prudent navigation but the safety of a
vessel depends ultimately on the judgement
of the navigator who should assess all
information, published or unpublished,
available to him.

This work has been corrected to
October 2006

Printed in Great Britain by
Imray Laurie Norie & Wilson Ltd

KEY TO SYMBOLS USED ON THE MAPS

Scale approximately 3'' to a mile

	Moorings
	Slipway
	Direction of stream
	Post Office
	Telephone
	Lock
	Weir
	Information
	Pump out
	Toilet
	Public House
	Fuel
	Water
	Church
	Station
	Showers
	Power Cable
	Footpath
	Winding Hole

ACKNOWLEGEMENTS

Grateful thanks are extended to the
Environment Agency and the Peterborough
IWA, in particular Michael Slaughter, for
their input.

RIVER NENE NAVIGATION

The River Nene is a particularly important navigation as it links the Grand Union Canal to the Middle Level and the sea. Although the navigation was originally commercial it is now almost entirely used for recreation.

Flowing through Northamptonshire, Cambridgeshire, Lincolnshire and bordering Norfolk, the Nene gives contrasting views of eastern England. In Northamptonshire the river flows through farmland and the industry of Northampton, Wellingborough and Irthlingborough interspersed with the numerous stone villages with their churches for which this 'county of squires and spires' is famous.

Peterborough dominates the route through Cambridgeshire with the cathedral visible on the horizon across the fenland landscape. The Nene was tidal to Peterborough until the construction of the tidal lock and sluice at the Dog-in-a-Doublet in 1937.

The tidal Nene continues to flow through Cambridgeshire to the busy port of Wisbech with its Dutch style waterfront architecture and the port at Sutton Bridge before entering the Wash between two towers known as 'the lighthouses'.

Rising at sources near Badby and Naseby, the Nene becomes navigable at Northampton where these tributaries combine. Navigation begins at the junction with the Northampton Arm of the Grand Union Canal near Cotton End Lock and extends 88 miles (141km) to the sea.

The Environment Agency's Recreational Waterway stretches from Cotton End Lock Northampton to Bevis Hall, just upstream of Wisbech. River users must conform to the Agency's Recreational Byelaws throughout this length.

Boat traffic is increasing on this attractive waterway but it is still quiet compared with other navigations such as the canals and Great Ouse.

A speed limit of 7mph (11kph) applies throughout the navigation except for one mile downstream of Peterborough. This derestricted stretch is clearly signposted.

There are 68 fixed bridges and 37 locks between Peterborough and Northampton. Each lock is 83ft 6ins (26m) long and 15ft wide (4·6m) with a minimum depth of 4ft (1·2m). To make allowances for adverse conditions, the maximum, dimensions for craft should be regarded as:

Length 78ft (23m)
Beam 13ft (3·9m)
Draught 4ft (1·2m)
Headroom 7ft (2·1m)

All craft approaching these maximum dimensions would have difficulties.

Water levels cannot be guaranteed. Care should be taken when:

1. Approaching any of the river controls, weirs, sluices, locks etc, should there be any significant flow on the river.

2. Stopping overnight, or leaving a boat for a considerable length of time – i.e. over winter (where boats are permitted to remain in the water) – or in a flood situation, do not moor in shallow water or with a tight rope or chain as water levels may fluctuate. If the level drops and a craft is moored aground or in shallow water, it may be damaged. If the level rises and mooring ropes or chains are tight, the boat may take on water, be pulled under or even broken free. The Environment Agency (Anglian Region) disclaims liability for any damage caused to craft moored on the river, as a result of fluctuating water levels.

BOAT LICENSING AND REGISTRATION

Registration with the Environment Agency is required before craft can use the River Nene and details of regional requirements for the registration and licensing of craft to use the waterways described in this booklet are available from:

River Nene

Environment Agency
Anglian Region
Kingfisher House
Goldhay Way
Orton Goldhay
Peterborough PE2 5ZR
☎ (08708) 506506
www.environment-agency.gov.uk

Boat owners navigating Recreational Waterways within the Environment Agency's Anglian Region should acquaint themselves with the following legislation, copies of which can be obtained from the Environment Agency at the above address.

The Anglian Water Authority Act 1977.

The Recreational Waterways (Registration) Byelaws 1979

The Recreational Waterways (General) Byelaws 1980

RIVER NENE

Northampton to Peterborough

Distance 57.3 miles (92.2km)
Length 78' (23.7m)
Beam 13' (3.9m)
Draught 4' (1.2m)
Headroom 7' (2.1m)
Locks 37

GRAND UNION CANAL
Northampton Arm
Gayton to Northampton
Distance 4.8 miles (7.7km)
Length 72' (21.9m)
Beam 7' (2.1m)
Draught 2' 6'' (0.8m)
Headroom 7' (2.1m)
Locks 17

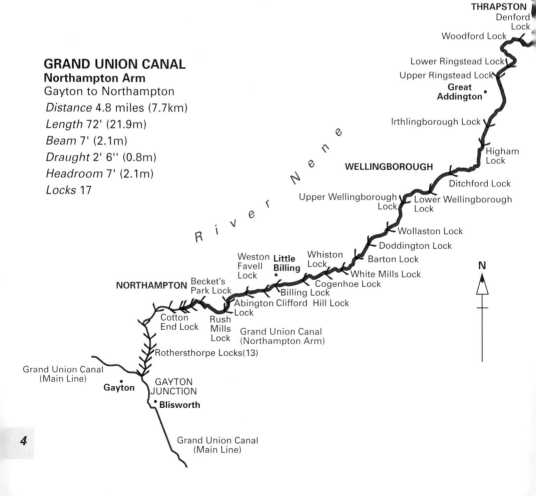

4

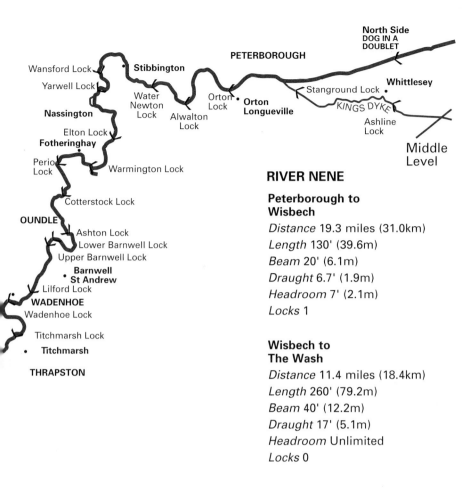

North Side
DOG IN A
DOUBLET

PETERBOROUGH

Wansford Lock
Yarwell Lock
Stibbington
Whittlesey
Stanground Lock
Water
Newton
Lock
Orton
Lock
Orton
Longueville
KINGS DYKE
Nassington
Alwalton
Lock
Ashline
Lock
Elton Lock
Fotheringhay
Middle
Level
Perio
Lock
Warmington Lock

RIVER NENE

Peterborough to Wisbech

Distance 19.3 miles (31.0km)
Length 130' (39.6m)
Beam 20' (6.1m)
Draught 6.7' (1.9m)
Headroom 7' (2.1m)
Locks 1

Cotterstock Lock
OUNDLE
Ashton Lock
Lower Barnwell Lock
Upper Barnwell Lock
Barnwell
St Andrew
Lilford Lock
WADENHOE
Wadenhoe Lock

Titchmarsh Lock
Titchmarsh

THRAPSTON

Wisbech to The Wash

Distance 11.4 miles (18.4km)
Length 260' (79.2m)
Beam 40' (12.2m)
Draught 17' (5.1m)
Headroom Unlimited
Locks 0

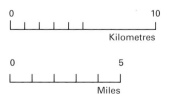

0   10
Kilometres

0   5
Miles

Grand Union Canal

British Waterways
Marsworth Junction
Watery Lane
Marsworth
Tring HP23 4LZ
☎ (01442) 825938

Mooring

Boats must not be moored within 36m of any locks, sluices, weirs or water intakes except when navigating through a lock. In some cases such as the Dog-in-a-Doublet, Bedford Road Sluice (Northampton) and Weston Favell (Northampton) mooring is prohibited for 100m on both sides of the structure.

River Nene locks

The majority of River Nene locks have steel pointing doors at the upstream end and vertical gates at the lower end. Some are now electrically operated.

Locks should be left with the pointing doors closed and the vertical lift gate raised and locked.

The vertical gates are normally locked. Keys are therefore required to operate the locks on the River Nene. These can be obtained from the Environment Agency, Anglian Region, Income Dept. 311, PO Box 263, Peterborough, Cambs PE2 8TD. Two weeks should be allowed to process applications. A windlass to fit a 1¼ inch square is required to operate the paddles.

Using the locks

The vertical steel gates should be operated with care. Children should not be allowed to operate them. Boat owners are advised to use side fenders when inside the lock pen, to avoid damage on the mooring chain.

Procedure when entering the lock from the higher level
- Lower the vertical gate
- Open paddles in the pointing doors
- Open the pointing doors when water levels are equal, and enter the lock
- Lower the paddles and close the pointing doors
- On manually operated locks raise the vertical door a few inches only. This is stiff at first, to prevent rapid opening of the door and possible boat damage. The vertical gate should be *fully raised* once the water level in the lock pen has fallen. The powered locks automatically allow two minutes for water to level.

Procedure when entering the lock from a lower level
- After entering the lock, lower the vertical gate
- Open paddles in the pointing doors
- When levels permit, open the pointing doors
- After leaving the lock, lower the paddles and close the pointing door
- Finally, *raise the vertical gate fully*.
- Do not moor within the yellow zones of the lock pen.

Caution If the pointing doors are found chained back (open) and the vertical gate partially lifted, ie the lock is 'reversed', no attempt to navigate should be made. Warnings are sited upstream and downstream of locks to indicate when a lock is reversed.

Should there have been heavy rain in the area it is probable there will be a rapid change in water condition eg rise in level, increase in current, change in colour. With any such change in conditions the Agency will almost certainly be operating sluices to regulate water levels and extreme care should be taken when approaching locks or other structures.

Useful telephone numbers and websites

Association of Nene River Clubs
www.ancr.org.uk

British Waterways, Blisworth, Northampton ☎ 0800 4799947

Dog-in-a-Doublet Lock
☎ 01733 202219 (Mobile 07887 831883)

Environment Agency Control Room
☎ 0800 80 70 60

Environment Agency National Enquiries ☎ 08708 506506

River Nene Inspectors
Northampton to Upper Wellingborough
Andy Hall ☎ 07760 422263
Lower Wellingborough to Lilford
Brian Hill ☎ 07768 171256
Upper Barnwell to Wisbech
Roy Smith ☎ 07714 064034

Environment Agency Office, Kettering
☎ 01536 385178

Flood Line ☎ 0845 9881188 – Quick dial 032112

Inland Waterways Association
☎ 01923 711114
www.waterways.org.uk

Jim Shead's waterways infomation site
www.jim-shead.com

Middle Level Commissioners, March
☎ 01354 653232
www.middlelevel.gov.uk
Northampton County Council
☎ 01604 236236
Port of Wisbech, Wisbech
☎ 01945 588059
Peterborough Unitary Authority
☎ 01733 563141
Stanground Lock-keeper, Peterborough
☎ 01733 566413
**Tourist Information – East
Northamptonshire Council**,
Oundle ☎ 01832 274333/273326
Tourist Information, Northampton
☎ 01604 622677
Tourist Information, Peterborough
☎ 01733 452336

Local Police Stations

Northamptonshire ☎ 01604 700700
Oundle ☎ 01832 274999
Wellingborough ☎ 01933 440333
Cambridgeshire ☎ 01480 456111
Peterborough ☎ 01733 563232

Slipways

Billing Aquadrome ☎ 01604 408181
Frontiers Activity Centre
☎ (01933) 651718
Ken Yates Marine Sales, Billing
Aquadrome ☎ 01604 408312
Middle Nene Cruising Club (available for club members)
Northampton Boat Club (available for club members)
Oundle Marina ☎ 01832 272762
Peterborough Boating Centre, 73 North
Street, Stanground, Peterborough
☎ 01733 566688
Peterborough City Council (Public
Slipway), Embankment Town Quay,
Peterborough ☎ 01733 563141 (office hours)
Peterborough Cruising Club
☎ 01733 232739
Peterborough Yacht Club (available for club members)
Willy Watt Marina, Ringstead ☎ 07710 094081

Short-term points and lock key agencies, River Nene and Grand Union Canal

Alvechurch Boats, Gayton Marina,
Northampton ☎ 01604 858685
Anchor Cottage Crafts (Licences), Long
Buckby, ☎ 01327 842140
Grand Junction Boat Co, Northampton,
☎ (01604) 858043
Ken Yates Marine Sales, Billing
Aquadrome, Northampton
☎ 01604 408312 (lock keys only)
Mike Wright, Dog-in-a-Doublet Sluice
Bungalow, Peterborough ☎ 01733
202219 (visitor licences)
Peterborough Boating Centre, 73 North
Street, Stanground, Peterborough
☎ 01733 566688

Other marine services

Princess Yachts and Marine Sales,
☎ 01604 890559
Classix ☎ 01604 891333
Cogenhoe Mill, Northampton
☎ 01604 890579
Oundle Marina, Oundle
☎ 01832 272762
Yarwell Mill, Stamford
☎ 01780 782247

Books

Alderton, D, Booker, J, *Batsford Guide to Industrial Archaeology of East Anglia*
Anon *Some Considerations of the River Nene running from Northampton to Peterborough and so to the Sea showing the feasibility and conveniency of making it navigable* (Cambridge University Library)
Asher, S J, *The River Nene Navigation*
Astbury, A K, *The Black Fens*
Bays, J, Russell, R, *Canals of Eastern England*
B B, *A Summer on the Nene* (D Watkins-Pitchford)
Cambs Federation of WI, *Cambridgeshire Village Book*
Cligman, J, Crowe, N, *Hertfordshire to Norfolk*
Dean, C & V, *Notes for First Time Boaters on the River Nene*
East Northamptonshire District Council, *East Northamptonshire Visitor Guide*
Environment Agency Brochure, *The Nene*
Environment Agency, *Rivers Great Ouse and Nene Navigation Notes*
Flag Fen Bronze Age Excavations
Hammond, C W, *Tracing the History of Place Names*

The River Nene

7

Heritage House Group Ltd, *Elton Hall and Gardens*

IWA Peterborough Branch, *Hereward Magazine*

Jenkins, H J K, *Along the Nene*

Jones, J, *A Human Geography of Cambridgeshire*

Lord Orford's *Voyage round the Fens 1774* (Intro A S K Jenkins) Mary Liquorice notes (Cambs Libraries Publication)

Muir, R, *The Villages of England*

The National Dragonfly BioMuseum Pamphlet

Nene Valley Railway, *Visitor Guide and Timetable*

Northamptonshire County Council, *Countryside for Everyone*

Northamptonshire County Council, *Countryside Walks*

Environment Agency. *Preferred Option for Northampton Flood Defences*

Environment Agency *The Nene Navigation*

Environment Agency *River Nene Waterway Plan*

Northampton Borough Council/Environment Agency. *Northampton River Valley – Master Plan*

The Nene Valley Project – The Nene Way

Pearsons Canal Companion. *The Nene*

Perring, F. *A Guide to the Nature Reserves of Eastern England*

Peterborough City Council, *Peterborough 2002/03*

Peterborough Cathedral, *The Precincts Trail*

Pevsner, N, *The Buildings of England Bedfordshire Huntingdonshire and Peterborough*

Pevsner, N, *The Buildings of England – Northamptonshire*

Phillips. D, *The River Nene*

Speed, J, *Counties of Britain – a Tudor Atlas*

Taylor, C *The Cambridgeshire Landscape*

Ordnance Survey Landranger Sheets 1:50 000 *131, 141, 142, 152, 153* Second Series

Ordnance Survey Explorer Series 1:25 000 *223, 224, 227, 235*

Wells, W *Bedford Level*

Welland and Nene LFDC *Environment Agency Asset Improvement Programme*

Thanks are due to Irven Forbes, Sue Cant, Andy Hall, Roy Smith and the Nene Waterways Team at the Environment Agency Anglian Region.

Grand Union Canal. Distances in Miles

Gayton Junction,
junction with the Main Line to:

Gayton Marina	0.1
Milton Road Bridge No 3	0.5
Rothersthorpe Top Lock No 1	0.7
Rothersthorpe Bottom Lock No 13	1.7
Wootton Lock No 14	2.1
Hardingstone Lock No 15	3.0
Duston Mill Bridge No 13 and	
Hunsbury Hill Industrial Museum	3.3
Northampton Lock No 16	4.1
Cotton End Lock No 17, junction with	
River Nene	4.8

River Nene. Distances in Miles

Northampton, junction with Northampton
Branch of the Grand Union Canal to:

Northampton, South Bridge	0.1
Becket's Park Lock No 1	0.4
Rush Mills Lock No 2	1.6
Abington Lock No 3	2.0
Weston Favell Lock No 4	2.9
Clifford Hill Lock No 5	3.7
Billing Lock No 6	4.3
Cogenhoe Lock No 7	5.4
Whiston Lock No 8	6.5
White Mills Lock No 9	7.2
Barton Lock No 10	8.1
Doddington Lock No 11	8.8
Wollaston Lock No 12	9.9
Upper Wellingborough Lock No 13	11.2
A45 Bridge	11.3
Lower Wellingborough Lock No 14	12.1
Ditchford Lock No 15	13.9
Higham Lock No 16	15.9
Irthlingborough Bridge	16.3
Irthlingborough Lock No 17	16.8
Upper Ringstead Lock No 18	19.1
Lower Ringstead Lock No 19	19.7
Woodford Lock No 20	21.9
Denford Lock No 21	22.8
A14 Bridge	23.4
Islip Lock No 22	24.2
Titchmarsh Lock No 23	26.3
Wadenhoe Lock No 24	28.7
Lilford Lock No 25	29.7
Upper Barnwell Lock No 26	31.9
Lower Barnwell Lock No 27	32.3
Ashton Lock No 28	34.1
Oundle Bridge	35.0
Cotterstock Lock No 29	36.2
Perio Lock No 30	38.0
Warmington Lock No 31	40.4
Elton Lock No 32	42.0
Yarwell Lock No 33	45.0
Wansford Lock No 34	46.2
A1 Bridge	46.9

Waternewton Lock No 35	49.9
Alwalton Lock No 36	51.7
Orton Lock No 37	55.4
Peterborough Bridge	57.3
Peterborough, junction with Branch to Stanground and Middle Level Navigations	57.9
Dog-in-a-Doublet (inn) Lock No 38 (power-operated, with emergency hand operation)	62.5
Popley's Gull	64.2
Guyhirn	70.6
Bevis Hall	74.0
Wisbech Town	76.6
Junction with North Level Main Drain	81.9
Junction with South Holland Main Drain (sluice entrance is only opened at flood times)	83.2
Sutton Bridge	83.9
Guy's Head 'Lighthouses'	86.9
The Wash at Crabs Hole, mouth of river	88.0

For passage to and from the tidal River Nene

The river is tidal for 25 miles downstream of the Dog-in-a-Doublet Lock which is five miles below Peterborough. Registered craft may pass through this lock every day from 0730 hours until official sunset time. Boat owners are advised to telephone the lock-keeper at Peterborough ☎ 01733 202219, in advance of their arrival to make arrangements for passage.

For information in respect of the passage of craft or moorings in the port of Wisbech and down to the sea apply to:

The Port Manager
Port Office
Wisbech ☎ 01945 588059

Craft should proceed through Wisbech with care. The banks are lined with steel and concrete piling, there is stone in the bed, and there is a strong run on the flood and ebb tide, particularly at the lower stages.

Introduction

The Nene flows east to Northampton where it turns north through one of the pleasantest vales in that county to Wandsford, where its course is east to Peterborough, where it enters this fenny flat and divides itself into sundry branches

Wells *Bedford Level*

The River Nene has been described as the perfect river for the boating enthusiast, as its gentle current makes it generally safe and easy to navigate. While the trappings of civilisation are never too far away, the river often winds its course through wonderfully unspoilt areas. It is very much a river of contrasts. Not only does the pronunciation of its name change from 'Nen' to 'Neen' at (approximately) Thrapston Town Bridge, but the land through which it flows changes character completely once the A1 trunk road has been crossed. Upstream of this crossing, the Nene winds its course mainly through undulating uplands, able to expand into its flood plains, when the need arises. East of the A1, however, it is confined between the high embankments, which protect the surrounding flat fen lands from inundation by its waters. While of vital importance to the flood defence of the Fens, the presence of these embankments does render the river less interesting to navigators, particularly as the undulating, ridge and valley Nene of the uplands is replaced by the artificial straight cuts of the drainers.

The Nene Valley was formed about 10,000 years ago, at the end of the last Ice Age, from meltwater, as the ice retreated northwards. These waters ground through the soils to form the broad deep valley present today. The mud then deposited in time became the rich soil, ideal for grass growing and forming the fertile stock grazing lands for which the valley became famous. Sand and gravel deposits were formed, many now extracted for use in construction projects and leaving the legacy of the necklace of lakes which now adjoin the river. Agriculture still remains the predominant agricultural activity however, and 40% of the Nene catchment is classed as Grade 1 or 2 agricultural land by DEFRA.

The River Nene begins its life in the porous limestone hills of the south and west Northamptonshire uplands. All of the precise sources are hard to trace, for several small brooks can be said together to form the source and the very name 'Nene' is said to derive from 'nine', a reference to the nine springs said to give it birth. There are however, two major sources. The first rises close to Naseby, the site of the famous battle of the English Civil War where, in 1645, the tide of the struggle turned firmly in favour of Cromwell, while the second emerges into the light of day at Arbury Hill, near Badby. Northamptonshire has generally limited access to navigable rivers and was therefore more isolated in past times, than some of its neighbouring counties.

The two major sources of the river unite at Northampton, one of the two largest settlements on the Nene, from where they continue their journey to the sea as one. The navigable Nene begins at its junction with the Grand Union Canal and ends in the tidal waters of Crab Hole on the Wash. Along its course, the Nene is traversed by main rail links and major road crossings such as the M1, A5, A6, A14, A1 and A47.

Although, more recently, navigation of the Nene has become a leisure activity it was, in times past, a vital commercial artery. The Romans were probably the first to exploit the river, constructing a network of canals, for example, the Car Dyke, running from the Nene to Lincoln. Their influence can still be seen at various times in a journey along the river. The Vikings also used the Nene to penetrate inland but the river so familiar to those early explorers, a stream of gravels, fords and other crossing places, has now been substantially changed by man, even in the upper reaches, which are 'natural' in comparison to the fen stretches. In places little 'dead arms' of the river can still be seen, evidence of the twists, turns and oxbows that so marked the original course.

Until the eighteenth century, the accepted upstream limit of the Nene navigation was Alwalton, six miles upstream from Peterborough. Below Peterborough, the river was deeper and broader and seagoing ships could reach Wisbech from the Wash, if they managed to avoid the mudbanks. Often fen lighters were used for this, a type of craft believed to be descended from Viking ships, with up to five such vessels tied together; their single square masts hinged to permit passage under the low bridges, enabling them to take advantage of available wind power.

In 1478, Bishop Morton of Ely, who was politically connected with Margaret, Countess of Richmond, mother of Henry VII, instigated a navigation cut 40 feet in width by 4 feet deep from Peterborough to

Guyhirn, and this new Morton's Leam then became the main course of the river. Further improvements to the river between Peterborough and Wisbech were made two hundred years later by the Bedford Level Corporation, which took tolls from the commercial navigators who made use of their works.

As regards the Nene upstream of Alwalton, a pamphlet was produced in 1653, seeking financial backing for making the Nene navigable towards Northampton, by way of a scheme comprising of 33 locks, capable of taking vessels of between 8–10 tons, at a cost of £8000. While nothing came of this, an Act of Parliament was passed in 1713, to develop the river above Peterborough. However, this Act required that all of the river should be made navigable and no one came forward to take on the task. A second Act, passed in 1724, therefore sought to address this, by appointing Commissioners to bring the first Act into execution and enabling parts of the river only to be made navigable. Work therefore finally began and by the 1730s, the Nene was navigable as far upstream as Thrapston. In 1756, a further Act was passed to enable the navigation to be extended a further 25 miles towards Northampton and Yorkshire engineer John Smith was put in charge of the project. By early 1760, the navigation had reached Wellingborough. Northampton itself was reached on the 7th August 1761 amidst great celebration, when 38 barges, mainly carrying coal, came up to the wharf at the South Bridge. The navigation was initially a great success. Travel by water drastically reduced the price of coal and passenger traffic and pleasure boating became important, particularly bearing in mind the appalling state of the road network at that time.

The building of the Grand Junction Canal nearby, helped to reinforce the position of Northampton as a trading centre and this canal reached Blisworth in 1796. In 1815, following local pressure, a new Northampton spur was opened, connecting the canal to the navigable Nene. This however, had the effect of lessening the importance of the link to the sea, since it opened up access to the canal network of the Midlands. This, and especially the coincident growth of the railways, saw the commercial navigation decline, a position not helped by the general condition of the river, since comparatively little maintenance or improvement work was carried out. The Admiralty Papers of 1850 show the extent of the decline by including a survey of the Nene and indicating that 'various improvements could open up navigation upwards of 20 miles inland for certain classes of sea borne vessel' and enable coasters to reach Peterborough. The true condition of the Nene navigation was neatly summed up by George Day, solicitor to the promoters of, what became, the Nene Valley Drainage and Navigation Improvement Act 1852 as, 'the water is so little used (that a boater can) seldom find any horses to borrow to drag boats through the staunches.' The income from navigation tolls fell away and repair bills for the navigation grew. In 1909, a Royal Commission reported that navigation from Northampton to Wisbech was difficult for barges of the smallest size but even for those, it was impracticable in certain parts of the river. In 1920, a small motor launch attempted to cover the 58 miles by river between Peterborough and Northampton, but had to be dragged overland in places.

In the 1930s however, the River Nene Catchment Board improved the navigation by dynamiting shoals and the years immediately prior to the Second World War saw a brief revitalisation of commercial traffic. New locks were installed, the construction of the Dog-in-a-Doublet sluice pushed the tidal limit downstream and, in 1938, small seagoing vessels got as far upstream as Peterborough. Following the Second World War however, road building boomed and commercial boat traffic, the last of which served Wansford quarries and Whitworth's Mill at Wellingborough, effectively ended in the late 1960s. Coincident with this, however, social changes saw the growth in the use of the river as a leisure industry.

The navigable Nene stretches 88 miles from Northampton to the sea and is mainly controlled by the Environment Agency, from which a licence to navigate is required, unless reciprocal arrangements with another navigation authority exist. The most important of these arrangements is the Gold Licence, available from either the Agency or British Waterways, which permits craft licensed by either Authority to navigate the other's waters. An Environment Agency key is required for access to the locks, water points, sewage disposal points etc but the BW windlass fits the gate paddles. BW control the connection via the Northampton Arm of the Grand Union Canal to the Midlands Canal Network, while the Nene also links to the River Great Ouse system via the Middle Level Commissioners' waterways at Stanground.

There are 38 locks on the Nene from Northampton No.1 Lock now also known as Becket's Park Lock to Dog-in-a-Doublet, 31 of which comprise of guillotine gates on the downstream end of the locks and 25 of which at present, or by the end of the 2006 season, will have electrically operated guillotine gates. Boats of 13' beam or less should be able to navigate the whole length of the river. All of the locks, except Becket's Park were, until recently, of the unmanned guillotine type but following concerns over the safe operation of and vandalism at some locks, the Agency commissioned Halcrows in 2000, to produce a Lock Safety Review Report. This concluded that, while the locks were structurally sound, various hazards existed for lock operators/bystanders and that the standard of lock safety should be improved. A number of these structures have therefore been improved, thanks to extra government funding. The Agency's intention is to undertake a number of further lock improvements in the next few years and facilities although, at the time of writing, they have been advised of significant cuts in the funding provided by the Department for the Environment, Food and Rural Affairs for 2006/7 onwards, which will clearly have an impact on the ability of the Agency to deliver such improvements. In the winter of 2005/6, eight Nene Locks, Orton, Elton, Wadenhoe, Cottestock, Higham, Doddington, White Mills and Abingdon were drained down to allow repairs to be undertaken. The Agency are however currently assessing a number of sites for the construction of further facilities over the next two years, with the following sites/projects under consideration

a. One 48-hour mooring site to be chosen from:
   i Midsummer Meadow, Northampton downstream of Rushmills Road
   ii Upstream of Upper Wellingborough Lock
   iii extension of facilities on Wellingborough embankment
   iv At Wellingborough close to the Ise junction
b. Lengthen the existing 48-hour moorings at the Rushden and Diamonds site, Irthlingborough
c. Extending the existing 48-hour moorings by the Middle Nene Sailing Club downstream of Islip
d. The creation of 120 metres of 48-hour moorings at Oundle
e. The creation of 48-hour moorings downstream of Wansford Lock
f. The creation of 48-hour and steam boat moorings at Yarwell
g. Pump-out improvements at Wellingborough and Thrapston

In addition to the locks with electrically operated guillotine gates a further six have conventionally mitred top or bottom gates. The guillotine should be left in the up position after locking and requires between 90–150 turns to raise or lower, although the Agency are currently experimenting with a new prototype handle aimed at improving guillotine operation and a new paddle mechanism is being trialled, the first such installation being at Upper Wellingborough Lock in 2005.

Where the lock has a manual guillotine door, a lockable bolt retains the handle for the lock operation. This is released by inserting the Agency key. The bolt should be securely pushed into the operating wheel after use and the spring-loaded lock fully pushed home.

When the guillotine is raised, water flows over many of the top gates and in varying quantities. The Agency are however, investigating ways of reducing or eliminating water flowing over the upstream lock gates and hope shortly to have reduced this at 17 locks by fitting planks etc. There is also further work planned on some of the powered locks to reduce leakage and improve gate operation. Until such improvement are installed, however, it is recommended that vessels are securely roped, using a centre rope round a central bollard and a bow rope if going downstream. When locking upstream, the water coming over the top gates is often sufficient to fill the lock within a short time, thus avoiding the need to open the paddles.

Great care must be taken when opening the guillotines to proceed downstream. Boaters are advised to only make one or two cautious turns and wait until the lock is almost empty before raising the gate fully. Otherwise the vessel can be difficult to control if it surges forward.

The locks have bollards for use and ladders placed on the left-hand side, near the guillotine, when proceeding downstream and another near the mitre on the left-hand side when proceeding upstream.

The general speed limit on the Nene is 7mph and navigation with particular care is required when the river is in spate. The Environment Agency is working with the boat clubs and others along the Nene to raise awareness of safety considerations during times of high flow, when the Agency issue 'strong stream' advice. This provides warnings to river users of the procedure whereby navigation locks on the Nene at Doddington, Titchmarsh, Wadenhoe, Lower Barnwell, Cotterstock, Warmington, Elton and Yarwell are 'reversed' with the lock doors chained back and the guillotine doors raised, so closing them to boaters, when the lock is used to discharge flood water. The Agency have issued the following official guidance

Navigation Closures, Restrictions & Strong Stream Advice (SSA) Information

Navigation Closures and Restrictions

The Environment Agency posts advance information on closures and restrictions to the navigation of the river on the information boards at each lock. This information is also published on the Agency's website www.environment-agency.gov.uk/navigation and held by the marinas and boat clubs along the river.

Strong Stream Advice (SSA)

In times of high and fast flows some of the locks on the River Nene may be 'reversed', an operation whereby the locks are used to discharge flood waters and that closes the affected locks to navigation. The Agency offers a free Strong Stream Advice (SSA) service to tell boat users that locks are 'reversed' and that it is strongly recommended against attempting to navigate. No attempt should be made to pass through a lock if the mitre doors are chained back and the vertical gate is partially lifted. To receive SSA please contact the Agency's National Customer Contact Centre ☎ 08708 506 506 and ask to be added to the service. You can request to receive SSA by many different methods that include Automatic Voice Message, Text, Pager, Fax or Email. Please note that automated warnings can be generated any time of the day or night.

The following locks are reversed on the River Nene in times of high flows:

Doddington, Titchmarsh, Wadenhoe, Lower Barnwell, Cotterstock, Warmington, Elton, and Yarwell

When SSA is in force, signs to inform users on the River Nene are located at the top and bottom locks of the Northampton Arm of the Grand Union Canal, at Stanground Lock,

Peterborough, at the Dog-in-a-Doublet tidal lock, many of the moorings, all reversed locks, and some other locks. A number of boat clubs (in association with the Agency) raise red flags when SSA is in operation. These flags not only inform club members that SSA is on, but are of value to other river users as well.

River users can also telephone the Agency's Floodline Information Service to hear the recorded AVM which will inform users whether Strong Stream Advice is on or off. To do this complete the following steps:

1. Call Floodline ☎ 0845 988 1188. You will be welcomed to Floodline and offered different touch tone options
2. Choose option '1' to listen to pre-recorded information for flood warnings currently in force
3. Then simply enter the River Nene quick dial SSA number 032112 when prompted

The Nene is susceptible to a rapid rise after heavy rain, due to its nature and catchment area and river users are advised to pay close attention to weather forecasts.

Passage into the tidal river downstream of the Dog-in-a-Doublet sluice can be made by prior arrangement with the sluicekeeper. It should be remembered, however, that this stretch can be treacherous, especially during spring tides. The navigation of the Nene around the port of Wisbech falls under the control of the port authorities and downstream of Wisbech, under the control of the port of Sutton Bridge.

Water and sewage disposal points are generally rare on the river, but there are plans for more to add to the three new water points installed on a joint initiative between the Environment Agency and Anglian Water a few years ago. Public moorings too are relatively few in number and mooring is not allowed at landing stages or (save in the course of passage) adjacent to locks. However, as mentioned above, more short stay moorings are planned. There are also several low bridges on the system, with inverted gauge boards adjacent to them to give guidance on available headroom. The Agency are also installing booms adjacent to weirs as a safety measure. These are to be coloured green to 'blend in' better with their 'surroundings' and have already led to comments from users about potential visibility problems.

Environmentally, the Nene valley is an important route for migrating birds, situate as it is on the 'route' from the Humber estuary to the north and the Exe estuary to the south. The 'necklace' of lakes formed in the valley by the gravel extraction, together with the river and its flood plain, are important bird feeding and breeding areas and there are a number of important nature reserves close to the river.

The Nene Waterways Team are also working closely with British Waterways and Northamptonshire Police to introduce 'Boat Watch' a scheme aimed at reducing opportunities for vandalism, anti-social and other criminal activities on the Nene, which it is hoped to introduce in 2007.

Grand Union Canal — Northampton Arm

The harvest of the River is her revenue

Isaiah

This arm was built in the early eighteenth century and leaves the main canal at Gayton Junction (moorings, shop, water, WC). A towpath follows the west bank as far as the first minor road crossing, where the path crosses the canal to then follow the right bank; as the canal turns northeast to run close to the A43 trunk road. After a few hundred yards, Gayton Marina (Alvechurch) is reached ☎ 01604 858685 where water, pump-out facilities, moorings and fuel are available) after which the canal turns again, moving away from the A43, this time to the northwest, where it is crossed by a second minor road, at the Milton Road bridge before coming back to the northeast. After this point the first two Rothersthorpe locks are encountered in quick succession. Comments have been made by users that the positioning of the handrails on the Rothesthorpe Lock gates makes it awkward to step across to close the gates. There are 13 Rothersthorpe locks on this stretch of canal, as the gradient changes dramatically and quickly to meet the level of the River Nene. There are limited opportunities for mooring in this stretch and the boater is soon aware of the urban landscape of Northampton. After the first two locks, the canal is crossed by the Rothersthorpe Road leading to Rothersthorpe village where the thirteenth century church of St Peter and St Paul contains a late-sixteenth-century pulpit and refreshments are available at the Chequers PH on North Street (☎ 01604 830892) before it runs close again to the A43. The next three Rothersthorpe locks are passed in quick succession before a drawbridge

crossing, and then a further five before a second drawbridge crosses the flight. After Lock 11 the M1 slip road to junction 15A passes overhead. Lock 12 must be negotiated before the M1 itself passes overhead with the Rothersthorpe motorway services area, before the downstream slip road is reached. After the final Rothersthorpe lock is negotiated, there is a further drawbridge and the canal turns to the west, moving away again from the A43. Of the three drawbridges mentioned, however, two are chained open and the third is partially dismantled, awaiting refurbishment. The Rothersthorpe Road/ Banbury Lane bridge crosses just after Wootton Lock, already the fourteenth on the navigation and some half mile from the last Rothersthorpe Lock, is reached. The canal then passes a lake on the left bank before curving to the north east. At this point, the River Nene can be seen coming from the northwest to run parallel to the canal for a short distance before both are crossed by the A45 road bridge. The tower of St Crispin's Hospital, one of the landmarks of Northampton is visible from the canal path.

River Nene

The infant Nene flows north to Duston Mill where it is crossed by the footpath leading to the mill. Duston Mill reservoir, a balancing reservoir built to accommodate surface water drainage from new development to the west of Northampton and designed to be used for water-based leisure activities is located here, on the left bank. The Nene then turns east past the Sixfields Stadium, home of Northampton Town FC and is now accompanied in its journey by another infant, the Nene Way long distance footpath. This path, established by Northamptonshire County Council and continuing into Cambridgeshire runs in close proximity to the Nene for 70 miles from Badby. Here it follows the river on its right bank as it turns southeast and, then south, as the footpath from Hunsbury Lock links with the Nene Way. The Nene Way then crosses the Nene to run on the left bank. The river then turns east to join the Grand Union Canal and form the Nene navigation downstream of Northampton No.17 Cotton End Lock where there is also a connection to the Westbridge Arm of the canal and moorings on the right bank just upstream of the Lock. The northern and western branches of the Nene unite in the southwestern suburbs of Northampton just above the Town Bridge and almost opposite the junction with the Grand Union Canal.

Grand Union Canal

The navigation on the canal, after the A45 road bridge, is joined by the disused railway line which follows the course of the Grand Union as it turns through Hardingstone Lock, about 1 mile from Wootton Lock, where the footpath from Duston Mill crosses the canal. The canal and the adjacent Nene turn east and then southeast to pass by Hunsbury Hill Country Park on the right bank before the canal approaches Hunsbury Lock, some three quarters of a mile from Hardingstone Lock, where a footpath crosses the canal to head northeast and join the Nene Way alongside the Nene. The railway line still runs parallel to the navigation but the canal and river are next crossed by a second railway line heading northeast to Northampton Station. The canal then formally joins the River Nene at Northampton No.17 Cotton End Lock, a further three quarters of a mile on from Hunsbury Lock. The Grand Union Canal therefore connects the River Nene and its onward connections to the Midlands waterway network and in turn links that network to the Wash. The absolute upstream limit of the river navigation lies at West Bridge in Northampton Town. The maximum beam width for the Grand Union Canal is 7 feet. The navigation from the Grand Union Canal to Northampton Lock measures approximately 5 miles. The Gayton junction is 92 miles from the sea and 189 feet above sea level.

Northampton

Once through Northampton No.17 Cotton End Lock, the boater arrives at Cotton End. A new footbridge associated with and linking new developments crosses the Nene at this point. This was once a thriving commercial centre but is today being redeveloped as can be seen by the modern apartment buildings now constructed here on both banks of the river. This is part of the major regeneration of this part of the town, which will include the nearby Avon factory complex. Two major landmarks are in close proximity at this point. On the skyline is the 430 feet high tower built by Express Lifts, in 1982, to test new technology. The factory itself closed in 1997 but the tower remains and became recently the youngest listed building in England. The major landmark of the Carlsberg Brewery is the next in view, immediately on the left bank and just before the Northampton South Bridge crossing. Opposite the brewery is the Malt Shovel Tavern, on Bridge Street, ☎ 01604 234212. Brewing was always an important industry in the Nene Valley and this site is the former Phipps Brewery, which was redeveloped for Carlsberg in 1974. The complex comprises of 20 acres and being directly facing on to the river, is spectacular when lit at night. To facilitate the development, the northern branch of the Nene was diverted to join with the western branch 100 yards further upstream. The buildings were designed by Danish architect Knud Munk and won the 1975 Financial Times Award for Industrial Architecture.

The Nene was of course, in former times, very important for the transport of grain and, close to the South Bridge, still stands Latimer's and Crick's Grain Store. The Northampton River Valley Master Plan, drawn up in partnership between the Northampton Borough Council and the Environment Agency and involving a number of other organisations, proposes a marina development close to South Bridge as well as the enhancement of the neighbouring Becket's Park and Midsummer Meadow, although no funding is yet in place for this.

Becket's Park is on the left bank. Here there are moorings, including some for use by the disabled, incorporating a disabled access platform, although the river is embanked through the park and the view from such moorings is therefore restricted.

The park is named after Thomas à Becket, who was famously Archbishop of Canterbury between 1162–70 and was murdered in Canterbury Cathedral by Knights, who saw themselves as carrying out the wishes of Henry II. The problems between King and Archbishop had boiled over, at an earlier stage, at the Council of Clarendon in 1164, held at Northampton, when Becket escaped through a gate in the old town wall, the site being now situated in the northern corner of Becket's Park. There is also a well, known as Becket's Well, which tradition says is where he stopped for a drink during his flight. The park was formerly common land where freemen of the town were entitled to graze their cattle, hence the former name of Cow Meadow. It became a very popular public open space in Victorian times and is now a well used recreational area with tennis courts and bowling greens among its facilities. There is a public telephone at the main road junction near the traffic lights at the corner of the Victorian Promenade. The headquarters of Northampton Canoe Club are to be found on the left bank.

Just upstream of Becket's Park Lock the Nene splits, with the right hand southern channel looping round the south side of a lake lying between the two channels to rejoin the main channel in three distinct minor channels. A mural stands on the right bank of the Nene here, illustrating a river scene. The main Nene passes through Becket's Park Lock, one third of a mile from Northampton No.17, which was the last lock to be constructed, in 1761, and the first to be replaced, when the Nene navigation was modernised in the 1930s. It has pointing doors at each end. A lock key must be obtained from the Environment Agency to operate this lock as the standard key is of no use. As well as the moorings just mentioned, it is sometimes possible by arrangement to moor behind the island bordering the right side of the channel. Embarking at this lock can be difficult. In a joint initiative with Northampton Borough Council, the Agency had developed a safety centre at the corner of the boathouse facing Northampton Lock, with access being by way of navigation key. However, due to vandalism and other problems, this centre is closed and will not reopen until after development of the adjoining Avon site which is part of the town centre regeneration, but the timing of which rests with the West Northampton Development Corporation. The centre did and is intended to house a broad range of information about the Nene, with particular emphasis on safety for first time boaters. After Becket's Park Lock the river passes the sea cadets building on the right bank and then below two footbridges and care should be taken when passing under these. A footpath on the left bank then leads away into the centre of Northampton and Midsummer Meadows are now to be seen on the left side.

The Nene in and around Northampton is now much changed from its original state, due to successive drainage and flood defence schemes. In 1998 areas of the town and, in particular St James and Far Cotton, were seriously affected by flooding and a scheme by the Environment Agency to provide an improved level of protection for these areas to a 1 in 200 year return period (0·5% chance of flooding each year) has recently been completed. On the main channel itself in Northampton, channel widening up and downstream of the South Bridge has been undertaken. This included realignment of the bank opposite the Carlsberg Brewery, so that the northern arch of the South Bridge

has an unobstructed entry. In addition a River Nene Catchment Flood Management Plan is presently being prepared.

The Agency are, as mentioned earlier, developing a River Valley Master Plan with the Borough Council, to see how and the extent to which the flood defence improvements can act as a catalyst for riverside improvements and enhancements generally. The main object of the Master Plan is to 'enhance and conserve the river valley and surrounding environment and make it accessible to local communities and visitors so that they may fully appreciate its history and natural qualities.' Its intention (inter alia) is to enhance and protect the character of the river and surrounding open space, to promote appropriate leisure and recreational use of the river valley; to regenerate physically, economically and socially, the areas surrounding the river valley and to provide planning and design guidance for developers of the valley. So far as concerns navigation it specifically sets out to encourage use of the Nene and the Grand Union Canal (Northampton arm) by boats for recreational and commercial purposes and the provision of facilities, such as moorings, sanitary stations etc. in a secured environment. It points out that the undeveloped meadows of the flood plain surrounding the town play a vital role in protecting the urban areas and that development on those meadows should therefore be prevented so far as possible. The Plan has a 5−10 year implementation period and is likely to lead to other river valley projects.

The old course of the Nene also ran closer to the Bedford Road but this has been replaced by a newer, broader, deeper channel.

Northampton

People have lived in Northampton for over 5,000 years and excavation at Briar Hill in the late 1970s found a large circular earthwork enclosure, where Neolithic farmers held tribal ceremonies. By 1800BC the Nene Valley from here was an important trade route and also overlooking the town is Hunsbury Hill, whose name derives from 'bury' a fortified place and 'Hun' the name of a tribal leader, now partly covered by a modern housing development but also comprising a hill fort occupied by the Celts between 400BC–AD20 and later by the Saxons, who gave it its present name.

Hunsbury thrived under the Danes and became an important commercial centre, with the Viking public house providing a reminder of those times. The Romans founded a market town where Duston stands today and later the Danes made 'Northamtun', a base for their armies; the Anglo Saxon Chronicle recording that their army rode 'out of Hamtun to kill many men.' By the eleventh century, the town was referred to as 'Northhamtun', to distinguish it from 'Southhamtun', to which it was linked by an old route way. 'Hamtun' means homestead.

The town expanded rapidly after the Norman Conquest to become the third largest town in England by the time of its first extant Charter in 1189. Things were not always peaceful however. The walls were broken down by Henry III's army in 1264 and the town pillaged for its support of those rebelling against the King. The later Wars of the Roses saw Henry VI taken prisoner, following the Battle of Northampton which took place on the meadows on the south bank of the Nene on 10 July 1460 and the town was attacked by Prince Rupert's army during the English Civil War in 1643. There were also two great historical fires, in 1516 and 1675, the latter of which destroyed three quarters of the town. The rebuilt Northampton was however described by Daniel Defoe as 'the handsomest and best town in all this part of England'.

Northampton was built up on the shoe industry. Leather was important and available, with the Nene Valley providing rich cattle grazing and oak forests for tanning as well as the availability of water in the Nene itself. In 1213 there is the first written record of the footwear industry, a pair of boots being made for King John. By the middle of the sixteenth century, shoemaking was the largest craft and, one hundred years later, Cromwell engaged the Northampton workers to produce boots for his army. 150 years later, Northampton produced thousands of boots for the British Army during the Napoleonic Wars. Even so, the trade was comparatively small until the coming of the Grand Junction Canal, in 1815 and the railway in 1845. Between 1800 and 1900 the population increased from 7,000 to 87,000 and by the end of the nineteenth century, 40% of the adult population was employed in the shoe industry, a figure later reduced due to the availability of imports. In the middle of the now pedestrianised Abington Street, there is a bronze sculpture of two young children skipping across the tools of the shoemaker's trade, while the Northampton Central Museum and Art Gallery, on Guildhall Road, contains the world's biggest boot and shoe collection. The local football team, Northampton Town, are also nicknamed 'the Cobblers', in a reflection of the town's historic industry. Aside from the boot and shoe trade, the town contains a number of historic buildings, mixed with the modern. The gothic guildhall has a number of friezes depicting events from the town's history. The castle that once defended Northampton is however, long gone, demolished on the orders of Charles II, following his restoration, due to the support given by Northampton to the Roundhead cause, during the Civil War.

All Saints Church, although badly damaged by fire and rebuilt, with the help of a donation from Charles II, perhaps seeking to make amends for destroying the castle, still retains its thirteenth-century crypt, while St Peter, Mayfair has been described as the most interesting Norman Church in the county, with a number of unusual features e.g. angled buttresses and being constructed semi-circular in plan. It was constructed in 1170 and replaced an earlier Saxon church. Nearby, the remains of an early Saxon settlement have been discovered.

The seventeenth-century Sessions House still retains its splendid plaster ceiling by Edward Goudge and on London Road, stands an Eleanor Cross, one of three surviving crosses by John of Battle, with the stations being designed by William of Ireland, for which he was paid the princely sum of £3 6s 8d (£3.33). The poet John Clare (1793–1864) spent the last two decades of his life in Northampton. Known as the peasant poet, he wrote verse from the age of 13, inspired by his rural surroundings. His main works were 'Pocms descriptive of rural life' (1820) and 'The Shepherds Calendar' (1827). However, sadly, his stay in Northampton was due to the decline in his mental state and he was confined to the St Andrews Mental Hospital on the Billing Road. He is buried and a memorial stands to him, in Helpston.

As one of the two largest settlements on the Nene, Northampton has a good selection of shops, restaurants, hotels and other facilities.

Northampton to Wellingborough

A gentle but full stream flowing in placid beauty midst enamelled meadows
William Wells

The stretch of the Nene from Northampton to Wellingborough contains 14 locks and consists of 12 miles of charming countryside. Until comparatively recently, there was considerable narrow boat traffic on this stretch carrying grain between London and Whitworths' Mill at Little Irchester. The navigation here has a height restriction of 7'6"(2·3m)at the Nene Way footbridge. This refers to the headroom available at average summer water level. If water levels rise, restrictions may then have to be imposed.

At Midsummer Meadow where the Nene channel splits again, there are moorings, a water point, toilet, rubbish disposal facility and a pump-out adjoining the bridge to the Avon factory complex which, as mentioned, is due for redevelopment. There is a Morrison's supermarket across the road from these moorings. The Agency are considering installing further 48-hour moorings adjoining the Meadow downstream of Rush Mills Road. The minor left-hand channel which in part forms part of the original course of the Nene turns north, east and then north again to pass close to and then under the A5095 to Abington Mills before turning east again under the A45 to rejoin the main channel downstream of Weston Favell Lock. A footpath crosses Midsummer Meadow to cross this channel and then continues along both sides of the main channel, which itself turns southeast, past Barnes Meadow Local Nature Reserve on the left bank and crosses under the A45 road bridge. Once under the A45 road bridge, the Nene divides again. The northern left-hand channel is a flood relief channel and there is no entry for vessels. This is the entry to the Northampton Washlands Scheme created by the former Anglian Water Authority, a predecessor of the Environment Agency, to control floodwaters and protect development to the east of Northampton. The Washlands consist of channels and storage lakes and can hold up to 500 million gallons. The area has since become of national importance for large numbers of lapwing, golden plover and other migrating birds. The navigation channel turns south and then southeast. A footpath joins on the right bank.

Just upstream of Rush Mills Lock, which is just over a mile from Becket's Park Lock, is the Nene White Water Centre canoe slalom. The approach to this lock can however be difficult. It has a low entrance (7' headroom) and entry to the lock from upstream is greatly restricted on the right bank by a high fence. Rush Mills lock has pointing doors at each end and there is a public telephone available at the lock side. The Britannia Inn (meals, ☎ 01604 630437) stands adjacent to the lock.

After the Britannia Inn, a road bridge crosses the channel which then, just downstream, is crossed by the A428 at St Peter's Bridge which incorporates a pipeline crossing. The Nene Way footpath continues on the right bank as the channel turns north to Abington Lock; which has pointing doors at each end, some half mile from Rush Mills Lock. In the winter of 2005/6 the lock pen at Abingdon Lock was inspected following a drain down. Both upstream and downstream pintels were replaced to improve the operation of the doors together with other improvements round the lock, including new steps to improve access. The two channels of the Nene then rejoin, at the Abington Barrage Gate, an important flood defence structure, closed at times of flood. The channel then continues in a northeasterly direction.

The A45 trunk road runs close to the left bank for a short distance, before turning away to the northwest. The Nene Way continues along the right bank. For the next stretch between Abington and Weston Favell no mooring is allowed as the river widens out past the sluice leading into the flood storage washlands, on its approach to Weston Favell Lock and then, upstream of the lock, divides again, this time into three channels. There is no entry to the southernmost right-hand channel, with lakes on its right bank, but a footpath leads to Great Houghton (with its church St Mary's dating from 1754, Old Cherry Tree PH (meals, ☎ 01604 761399) and White Hart (☎ 01604 762940) on the High Street, telephone box by church) and north to Little Houghton (St Mary's, Post Office, Stores, Red Lion PH on the Bedford Road (meals, ☎ 01604 890661). There is still a pair of stocks to be seen in Little Houghton, southeast of the Church, on the Bedford Road. The navigable channel the centre of the three, turns east, but Weston Barrage Gate, a flood defence structure, prevents entry in times of flood. Weston Flavell itself has a shopping centre.

Weston Favell Lock, one mile from Abington Lock, comprises an electrically powered vertical gate, and the pointing doors have been refurbished. There is now an emergency mooring situated within the Washlands near to Weston Favell Barrage Gate. A telephone for use in emergency can be found in the building nearby and in an emergency help may be available from the Northampton Boat Club where there are members and visitors' moorings and the club house, downstream of the lock, on the left bank, although the slipway is for the use of members only.

After the Northampton Boat Club moorings the three channels rejoin. Here there is a sign warning those travelling upstream to keep right. Another set of lakes are passed on the right bank, while the Nene Way footpath from Weston Favell Lock has transferred to the left bank. A power line crosses the river and lakes are to be seen on the left side too, as the river approaches Clifford Hill Lock, three quarters of a mile from Weston Favell Lock. The river then divides again, with the southern channel being the Mill Race. At the mill is the Buglass Gallery and Coffee Shop (☎ 01604 890366) and the Clifford Hill Fortification on the right bank. This is one of the largest mottes in the country but there does not appear to be any historical record of a former castle and no bailey is apparent. It is instead a circular defensive mound probably built in the eleventh or twelfth century to control the crossing of a ford near a cliff (hence the name). The soil is however unstable and landslips on the south side may have led to its abandonment. The present flat top is said to be due to the construction of a bowling green there in the seventeenth century. Here the pleasant backwater has private moorings. There is a sign warning those travellers upstream to keep right. A footpath crosses the lock from Little Billing to the west to Little Houghton to the east. Views of Northampton are still possible looking upstream. Clifford Hill Lock is a vertical gate, electrically powered structure. The nearest public telephone is at Little Houghton by the village post office/stores, a good half mile walk from the lock. After Clifford Hill Lock, the river continues in an easterly direction past Billing Aquadrome (☎ 01604 408181) open March to November where there is a café, shop, restaurant, Millers Bar (the Quays) a visitor centre, water, moorings and a slipway as well as toilets, a cash point and a telephone but no pump-out facilities or fuel. Next to the Aquadrome are a Garden Village and a Discount Retail Shopping Outlet as well as a Premier Travel Inn and a luxury waterside lodge development. Billing Mill is mentioned in the Domesday Book and the Mill Museum is now part of the Billing Aquadrome complex. The present mill was built in the nineteenth century and worked commercially until the 1940s. It is now a public house (☎ 01604 415059). By the mill is a wide pool where moorings are available. Facilities are also available at the Riverview Bar and Restaurant just downstream of the mill (☎ 01604 891888). The Aquadrome comprises of 235 acres and was constructed after the meadows in this area were excavated for gravel, in the early twentieth century. It was landscaped by the then owner Mr Mackaness as 'a restful place for the public' and as a holiday venue and it contains a funfair and miniature railway. More recent developments on the site have included the creation of a caravan village and special events for instance, vintage car rallies, are frequently held. The Aquadrome is reached by a cut to the left just below Billing Lock. Here too is Ken Yates Marine Sales, where there is a slipway for vessels up to 2½ tonnes (☎ 01604 408312) and Billing Lakes are also well stocked with carp.

After the Aquadrome, Hardingstone Dyke joins on the right bank and the river turns northeast to Billing Lock, some half mile from Clifford Hill Lock. Billing Lock has an electrically-powered vertical gate. Nearby also are the villages of Great and Little Billing. Great Billing has the church of St Andrew, which possesses a twelfth century Norman nave and a post office building dated 1703. To the south of Little Billing is Delapré Abbey, the site of one of only two Cluniac monasteries in England.

The Nene Way footpath changes to the right bank downstream of the lock and then moves away from the river bank to follow the road to Cogenhoe. At nearby Ecton, lived Thomas Franklin, uncle of Benjamin Franklin.

The road from Little Houghton to the A45 crosses the river downstream of Billing Lock and just upstream of this are the premises of Princess Yachts which had a chandlery, although this has now been discontinued (☎ 01604 890559). The river flows past a gravel pit on the left, before dividing again into two. The minor northern channel rejoins downstream of Cogenhoe Lock passing by two gravel pits en route. It is crossed by a small stone bridge built around 1800 and recently refurbished by the Nene Valley

Project and Northants Heritage. This channel may have formed part of the old course of the Nene. The main channel turns southeast and then east and is crossed by the road bridge to Cogenhoe and then immediately afterwards by a footbridge, before turning northeast towards Cogenhoe Lock, where the guillotine gate is electrical, just over a mile from Billing Lock, where there is a sign advising those travelling downstream to keep left.

Here the river divides again. The backwater turns south and then southeast past gravel workings to the village of Cogenhoe, (pronounced Cook-no). The name originates from the hoe (hill) of Cugga, the Anglo Saxon owner of the manor. Here the twelfth century church of St Peter has an effigy of Nicholas de Cogenhoe who died in 1280, in the south aisle. A footpath to the village leads off from the backwater, and this then rejoins the main channel downstream of the lock. A second backwater, a little further north joins the first. A telephone is available (but normally only for emergency use) at the Cogenhoe Mill caravan site but there is a postbox on the road to the village and fifty yards or so further on, is a small village post office/shop. There is a pub, the Royal Oak (☎ 01604 890125), in the village over the level crossing, going up the hill. At the caravan site on the right bank downstream of the lock, there are showers and at the Chalet Village (☎ 01604 890579) a shop, private moorings and water and so far as space permits, visitors' shower, toilet and elsan emptying facilities. There are also some 'de facto' unofficial public moorings on the adjoining field. At Cogenhoe the right bank feels as if it is converging on you but the feeling passes as the river moves on to Whiston Lock.

The Nene Way footpath rejoins the bank side firstly of the more southerly channel after the Cogenhoe road and then runs alongside the right bank of the main channel, which continues to flow east and then northeast, past lakes on the left bank towards Whiston Lock one mile further on. Upstream of the lock, the river divides again, the backwater flowing around the lock to the north, over a weir, to rejoin the main channel downstream of the lock.

A second more minor backwater branches off further downstream, just before the lock. The scenery both up and downstream of Whiston Lock, which now has an electrically powered guillotine gate, is very pleasant and it has been described as 'standing in splendid

isolation at the centre of the Nene Valley'. This and White Mills Lock, a further mile downstream are seemingly close to but in fact isolated from, the village and stately home of Castle Ashby, the home of the Marquis of Northampton, which lie just under 2 miles away. This Elizabethan mansion has parkland designed by Capability Brown, as well as Victorian gardens. The house can be reached by a footpath through the grounds. The church of St Mary, in Whiston village, stands on its own on a hill overlooking the settlement and is only accessible on foot. It contains a sixteenth-century monument to its builder, Antony Catesby. The nearest telephone box to Whiston Lock is in Whiston village, which is a long walk from the lock. The nearest postbox is in the wall by the bus stop. There are no shops in Whiston.

Earls Barton

The Nene Way here crosses Whiston Lock and continues along the B573 to Earls Barton following the road through the village and turning to the south to rejoin the Nene after the eastern edge of Earls Barton, at Earls Barton Lock. A footpath, however, continues along the right bank. Earls Barton is a sizeable settlement with a full range of facilities. The Boot Inn (☎ 01604 810640) and Stags Head (☎ 01604 810520) stand just after the centre of the village on the right while just over a mile away, on the left, is the Saxon west tower of Earls Barton Church, All Saints, which is decorated with raised vertical stripes. This tower is regarded by many as the finest Saxon tower in England and is believed to have been once used as a lookout. The Church was enlarged by the Normans and in 1972, it featured on a postage stamp. To the north of the churchyard is the motte of the Norman castle. The village was referred to as Buartone in Domesday (meaning 'grange'), and there are two stories concerning the Earl referred to in the present name. One says it is David, the twelfth-century Earl of Huntingdon, while the other, probably more likely, refers to Simon de Sentis, who was Earl of Northampton and owned the manor in the twelfth century. Earls Barton was once an important leather tanning location and the Barkers' Shoe Factory, which began here in 1880, still produces about 250,000 pairs of shoes each year. At the square, is the Museum of Local Life which has a collection of industrial and domestic memorabilia.

Close to Earls Barton on the Mears Ashby-Washbrook road is Sywell Country Park (☎ 01604 810970). This 68-acre site is a former reservoir, previously used to supply water to Rushden and Higham Ferrers.

Downstream of Whiston Lock, the river is crossed by a farm bridge, at which point the footpath crosses to the left bank of the river. The river then loops South before turning back east on its approach to White Mills Lock, half a mile downstream of Whiston Lock. There are two small backwaters and a larger backwater channel that runs southeast, bypassing the lock. This has a weir at its entrance. Signs warn that it is advisable to keep to the left on the main channel when travelling downstream. Just upstream of the lock are moorings on the left bank. The guillotine door is now electrically powered. There is no telephone at the lock, but in an emergency, calls can be made from the nearby Garden Centre. There are however facilities at Earls Barton, which lies just over a mile from White Mills Lock. There are canoe launch points close to the lock.

Just downstream of the lock, the river and side channels are crossed by Station Road, leading to Dunkleys Restaurant and pub on the right bank (☎ 01604 810546) and Earls Barton to the left. After White Mills lock, there is no footpath adjacent to the bank as the river turns southeast under two bridges and past large gravel pits on both banks which form thickly populated waterfowl sanctuaries. After the first pit on the left bank, the river zigzags northeast and then straightens at the junction with the Barton Mill Race to flow in a straight northeastern channel to Earls Barton Lock which is one mile from White Mills. There is a large gravel pit on the right bank now. Because of the turns of the river, Earls Barton with its facilities remains relatively close, about one and a half miles away, but without easy access from this point. There is a canoe launch point at the lock.

Moving downstream, the valley becomes wider and the scenery more interesting. A track from the northwest past the mill carries the Nene Way from Earls Barton to cross the river at the lock and run along the right bank. A power cable then crosses the Nene.

The river continues to flow northeasterly past further gravel pits and the route of a conveyor belt for the sand and gravel pits on its right bank. The mill tributaries join from the left and the Nene then turns south, northeast and south in quick succession before turning northeast again past another large gravel pit on the right bank. There is a weir at the junction with a backwater which joins the right bank at this point and a sign advising boaters travelling downstream to keep left. The mill race from Hardwater Mill joins on the right bank, just upstream of Doddington Lock, which now has an electrically operated guillotine gate.

Doddington Lock is approximately half a mile from the main road and from Earls Barton Lock and a right turn at the crossroads along the B573 leads to Great Doddington village, which can also be accessed from the Nene Way. The village stands high on a hill, overlooking the valley, from which the broad reach of the Nene can be appreciated. It has a post office, shops and a telephone box near the Stags Head (meals, ☎ 01933 222316). The houses in Great Doddington reflect the local architecture of this part of the Nene Valley with grey limestone walls and red-tiled roofs. Due to the extensive gravel extraction in this area, some significant archaeological discoveries have been made. At nearby Wollaston, evidence of a Roman vineyard has been uncovered and a Roman road led out of the vineyard which itself contained an Anglo Saxon grave. The grave contained an iron sword and a bronze hanging bowl with hanging rings and decorated with round glass discs. The most significant discovery however, was an iron helmet with a boar's crest, indicative of the high status of the wearer.

The disused railway line runs close to the right bank at this point. A minor road bridge carrying the road between Wilby-Wollaston (Hardwicke Road) crosses the Nene downstream of the lock at which point the Nene Way crosses the river to move away on the left bank in the direction of Great Doddington. A minor footpath continues for a little way along the left bank as the mill race/backwater joins the main channel downstream of the lock. The river then curls east, is crossed by a footbridge and then flows past Summerleys Nature Reserve (☎ 01604 236633) home to large numbers of birds particularly tree sparrows and of dragonflies, on the right bank. Within this reserve, there is a circular walk and four bird watching hides with wheelchair access. A further backwater joins the river at a weir and two minor backwaters flow downstream from the weir and rejoin the main Nene downstream of Wollaston Lock, (one mile from Doddington Lock). Wollaston Lock now has an electrically powered guillotine gate. A footpath crosses the lock to run to Great Doddington via Hardwater Mill on the left bank, in which it is believed that Thomas à Becket hid after fleeing Northampton. There is a small community clustered around the mill, which is now a residence. This area forms a charming little islet amidst crowding willows and soft meadows. There are landing stages adjacent to the lock, which has superb surrounds. The right-hand channel should be taken by the mill.

From Wollaston Lock downstream the Nene winds a sinuous course, through beautiful country. The contours do not fall so obviously now as the change in gradient is slower than in the upper reaches.

Just before the backwaters rejoin the main channel, the Nene Way, which has travelled via Great Doddington, returns to run along the left bank. A power cable crosses the Nene, which then turns northeast past the bland architecture of HM Prison, Wellingborough. There is a pipe crossing, before a weired backwater which traverses Upper Wellingborough Lock. Upstream of Wellingborough the willow girt towpath gives the feel of a park like walk. The Nene Way continues along the left bank as the river flows past more water-filled old gravel workings to Upper Wellingborough Lock, which lies approximately half a mile upstream of Wellingborough Bridge and one and a quarter miles from Wollaston Lock. The Agency are considering installing 48-hour moorings upstream of Upper Wellingborough Lock. After the lock, the river crosses quickly under two road bridges carrying respectively the A45 and the A509. After the first of these is the Whitworths Victorian Mill built in 1866. Downstream of Whitworths Mill, the right bank becomes more natural while the left bank as it reaches the Wellingborough Embankment has mooring rings in the bank wall, with special portable blocks placed back from the pavement to be moved into position as required for mooring points. Little Irchester is on the right bank at the junction of the A45 and the A509, (Mills Road bridge). There is a large Tesco store on a roundabout on the A509 on the left bank, a little way along that road.

Little Irchester

Little Irchester has Iron Age traces and was an important Roman town which guarded a ford which then existed across the Nene. There is also a visitor centre outside of which can be seen the remains of a Roman coffin lid. In the early twentieth century, the town was very economically active, standing at the junction of two main roads and being near to the iron ore quarry and river wharf. However, the closure of the quarry and the wharf turned it into a quiet backwater. The All Hallows Church, now a fourteenth century building but formerly occupied by monks, is however of interest. The weather vane on the Church of St Catherine, depicts the Catherine Wheel, the torture instrument on which the saint met her death. The B573 also runs close to the left bank here as the river turns north and then east to cross the old railway bridge and pass a large lake on the right bank and a little further along the A509 towards Wellingborough is the Dog and Duck public house (☎ 01933 278606).

Here on the outskirts of Wellingborough, by Little Irchester, the Nene's largest tributary, the Ise, joins the main channel. The Environment Agency are considering installing a 48-hour mooring at this point. This tributary rises near Naseby and although often small in summer, can become a real torrent in winter. At this point too, close to the B570 and on the right bank, is Irchester Country Park. The Nene Way which had followed the left bank of the river to Little Irchester, then crosses the river at the A509 bridge before moving away east into the park. This Northamptonshire County Council reserve (☎ 01933 276866) consists of old ironstone workings, woodland areas and nature trails as well as scrub, grassland, dry slopes and wet dales. The first part of the Nene Way through the park follows the route of the old ore railway line. In the 1930s and 40s the area was planted with a large number of trees and its 200 acres are particularly well known for conifers and limestone plants. It attracts sparrow hawks and woodpeckers in particular and the grounds also contain a railway museum. Between Upper and Lower Wellingborough Locks, the Nene is crossed by the route of a disused railway. A backwater joins from the left bank flowing into the Nene just upstream of Lower Wellingborough Lock. Upper and Lower Wellingborough Locks are about a mile apart and are accessible with the standard Environment Agency Nene lock key. The lower lock has the shallower lift with a parapet on the right hand side projecting and care must be taken when approaching the lock. Users also report that the walkway on the upstream gate projects awkwardly, a problem unless both gates are opened. There is a toilet block on the Wellingborough Embankment set back from the river on the road and also a water point on the river side which again can be accessed by the standard Agency key and some 50 yards of moorings, refurbished by Wellingborough District Council together with an 'unofficial mooring area' by the Embankment Wall. The space available in this area however, has now been restricted by the presence of large rocks placed by the council to stabilise this wall which were moved by high flood flows in 2004. Discussions over a long term solution between the council and the Environment Agency are continuing. Signs have been erected confirming where mooring is no longer permitted on this stretch. The Agency are, however, considering the installation of further 48-hour moorings facilities here and the provision of a pump-out/chemical toilet, . The Embankment has recently been refurbished and this included the installation of lighting. There is a postbox at the crossroads on the Irthlingborough road.

Wellingborough

Wellingborough town centre itself is about a mile from the river. The name has various possible derivations, 'Wendel's burg' being favoured by some but a more likely source is from the wells or springs for which the area was previously famous – and particularly the 'red well' and the 'white well', the former name due to the ironstone content of the water. The Embankment, named 'the Walks' is very attrtactive and is especially famous for the semi-tame mute swans, as well as flower beds, lawns and pathways. In 1201, King John granted Wellingborough the right to hold a weekly market and the town contains a public school founded in the reign of Richard II and some fine old buildings have been retained. In the 1600s Wellingborough became famous for its waters which it was said had healing properties and the wells are still indicated on the town's coat of arms. Queen Henrietta Maria, the wife of Charles I, was a visitor to the waters. By the early eighteenth century, lace making was the main industry, but this in turn was overtaken by boot and shoe making. The town grew with the coming of the railway and nearby iron ore extraction.

In 1886, J B Whitworth built a mill on the riverside and the canal and river were used to bring imported grain from London. This continued until 1969, when it became no longer economic. The mill still makes flour from mainly British wheat. The Hind Hotel on Sheep Street (☎ 01933 222827), provides excellent refreshment.

Wellingborough to Islip

The splash of a fish, the secret rumble of the mill,
the whisper of a wind in the willows and the lazy life of summer days.

BB

Between Wellingborough and Islip, there is a height restriction (at average summer water level) of 7'6" (2·25m).

The Nene is shallower in the two mile stretch between Lower Wellingborough Lock and Ditchford Lock and, on passing Lower Wellingborough Lock, the river meanders gently as it passes the edge of yet more former gravel pits. There is a caravan park on the left bank. Two power lines and a minor footbridge cross the river in quick succession here, followed by the footbridge leading to Chester House and the former Railway Inn on the right bank. At Chester House, the site of a Roman settlement, the Nene Way returns to cross and follow the left bank of the river. Nearby is a Roman burial ground. The railway line crosses the river at the imposing twin Wellingborough viaducts. These viaducts known as 'Fourteen Arches viaduct' have a span of 350 feet over the Nene and were opened in 1857. One line was built with an easier gradient for goods traffic, so the tracks have different alignments. The river then turns northeast and east flowing past lakes again formed by former gravel pits on both banks, Ditchford Lake on the right bank and a small stream inlet on the right bank before passing under a road bridge (Ditchford Bridge) crossing upstream of Ditchford Lock which has an electrified downstream radial gate. Just before Ditchford Bridge, the Nene divides again with the navigation following the southern section which, between the road bridge and the lock, is a straight canalised length. A weir leads into the more meandering northern channel. The Nene Way follows the bank of the northern channel until the Ditchford bridge. There has been a bridge at Ditchford since 1292. Ditchford was once very popular with local people who used to come here to swim and fish. The area was known as 'Ditchford on Sea', had its own railway station on the Northampton to Peterborough Line and ice creams etc. were sold from the railway crossing keeper's cottage. Ditchford Lock is the only radial type lock with radial gate and pointing doors. The lock operating handle is padlocked to the gantry upright. The fast flowing backwater close to the old factory is good for roach and bream. There is no telephone within easy walking distance of Ditchford Lock but in an emergency, the telephone at the Anglian Water Services Ltd's Broadholme sewage treatment works on the left bank just a little way downstream may be available. From Ditchford downstream to Lower Ringstead Lock some six miles distant, the scenery is not quite so pleasant.

Ditchford Lake continues on the right bank downstream of the lock. The next lake on this bank is now the headquarters of the Skew Bridge Ski Club and two more lakes are visible between the Nene and the A45. On the left bank Broadholme Sewage Treatment Works is reached, after which the river turns southeast, with a small weired side channel on the left bank leading to the gravel pits from which a conveyor belt crosses the Nene. The channel meanders generally southeast running now close to the A45, and then parallel to that road for a short distance, via an artificial cut. A footbridge crosses here, leading the Nene Way, which branches off here from the river through a small former gravel pit, on the right bank, to Higham Ferrers.

Higham Ferrers

Higham Ferrers is noteworthy for its connections with H E Bates, the author perhaps best remembered now for The Darling Buds of May, who spent much of his childhood at his grandfather's farm near the town. Its history, however, goes back many centuries. By the eleventh century, the settlement was known as Hecham from the Saxon 'heah' meaning 'high' and 'ham' 'homestead'. In the twelfth century, the manor passed to the Count de Ferariis and, by 1279, the name Higham Ferrers was in common use. Henry Chichele, Archbishop of Canterbury from 1414–43 was born at Higham Ferrers in 1362. He founded the town's grammar school in 1422, Chichele College, an evocative mediaeval building still standing in the High Street and Bede House which provided a home for elderly men who were paid 1d (½p approx) a day pension six years later. Their duty was to pray for the King and for the founders of the Charity. His statue is on the church tower. Higham

Ferrers market place has a fourteenth century market cross and ditches near the north side of St Mary's church are the remains of the moat of the old castle, built in the eleventh century by William Peverel. In 1266, this castle was granted by Henry III to his son, the Earl of Lancaster, but the castle only survived for another 250 years, much of its stone being taken for the building of Kimbolton House in 1523. A wall of the old dovecote, now in the grounds of the Green Dragon Hotel on College Street (☎ 01933 312088) remains however.

The town is still part of the Duchy of Lancaster and St Mary's is a grand building, with two naves and a superb spire which can be seen from some distance away, particularly if navigating upstream. The town also contains a number of fine old buildings, grouped around the Market Square, which has become an important conservation area and a fair mixture of shops and pubs etc.

The Nene however, turns away from Higham Ferrers and then flows generally northeast, meandering before being crossed at Kings Meadow Lane by the previously 'notorious' Kings bridge, constructed of steel and concrete with two angle irons which must be negotiated. The approach should be slow but work to raise the headroom on this bridge has, however, been undertaken. Here the Nene Way crosses the bridge and turns northwest to Irthlingborough, although a footpath branches off from this to return to the left bank of the river just downstream of Higham Lock which is two miles, by river, from Ditchford Lock. The previously stiff doors at Higham Lock were freed off during the 2005/6 winter. Downstream of Higham Lock the channel is narrow and twisting and weed can be prolific. At the top of a hill to the right is the ruined shell of an inn, guarding the site of a long disused ford, from which a lane leads up to the town. There is also here, close to the A45, the Northamptonshire Wildlife Trust Nature Reserve, a 10-acre site known for its open water and wildfowl. It is part of a 450-acre complex of worked out gravel pits. There is also good canoe access here from Wharf Road to the river. A minor backwater curls back to rejoin the Nene on the right bank close to this point just after the river crosses the site of the former railway line. The channel continues northeast and is crossed by the A6 High Road bridge. Just off to the left now is the famous Doc Martens shoe factory shop (☎ 01933 652000), where the famous footwear has been produced since

1960 (although production is being transferred overseas), and beyond that the football ground of Rushden and Diamonds FC. Here, navigation facilities have been provided, comprising showers, toilets, rubbish disposal, chemical disposal, water point and pump-out facilities and a mooring. These facilities are thanks to a partnership between the Environment Agency and the R Griggs Group Ltd, owners of the football club. Since the R Griggs Group also own the Doc Martens shoe factory, boaters can now visit the factory shop and site restaurant at the Diamond Centre during a stopover. At the present time, however, due to break ins and vandalism, the shower room is closed. However, it has been agreed that for a small fee, boaters can use the sports hall complex facilities. Enquiries should be made to the complex reception (☎ 01933 652000). The Agency are however, considering lengthening the 48-hour moorings. At the A6 Station Road sliproad bridge which next crosses the river, navigators are advised to use the largest arch. A minor channel from the gravel pits joins on the left. Shortly after this, on the right-hand side, there is a weired backwater to the southeast. The minor channel itself subdivides into two, one of which rejoins the main channel immediately downstream of Irthlingborough Lock. The other sweeps round to the south, circling and being bordered by gravel pit lakes before turning north to rejoin the main channel, ½ mile further downstream. The main channel continues north to Irthlingborough Lock, one mile from Higham Lock. The Nene here is flanked by a series of old gravel workings now flooded to form lakes on either side of the channel which begin just upstream of the lock and continue for the next mile. The Nene Way footpath approaches the main channel from Irthlingborough and continues on the left bank past the lock. At Irthlingborough Lock, where the guillotine gate is now electrically powered and just downstream of the structure, is the Northamptonshire Association of Youth Clubs camp site on the left bank, near where there is a telephone. Boaters are advised here to go slow, to avoid canoes and other river users. From here it is one mile to the centre of Irthlingborough, a town with a full selection of facilities.

Irthlingborough

The town dates from at least AD780 and the name Irthlingborough is said to be derived from 'Yirtlingaburg' (the fortified place of a ploughman). Irthlingborough is on the opposite side of the river from Higham Ferrers but is connected to it by two bridges. The first is a fourteenth century stone bridge and carved into its stonework are the crossed keys of Peterborough Abbey. Perhaps the monks of that abbey arranged for its building? On its ten arches are a variety of grooves worn in the stonework over the centuries by the ropes of the old bargemen. The second bridge is the more modern viaduct built in 1936, which carries the A6. Navigation of both of these bridges calls for careful positioning and awareness of the river currents. There is a small nature reserve, of just over an acre, here. It is well known for the great crested newt, and comprises a hedge and ponds originally caused by subsidence. John Pyel, a native of Irthlingborough and Lord Mayor of London in 1473, founded a college in the town and arranged for the building of the tower of St Peter's Church which was built mainly between 1225 and 1250 but was taken down and rebuilt at the end of the nineteenth century as it was found to be leaning. The tower stands forty feet from the nave and belongs to the College. The effigies of John Pyel and of his wife are in the church. The belfry tower was one of the College buildings and is connected to the church by a vestry. In the town centre there are the pubs Oliver Twist (☎ 01933 650353) and The Bull (☎ 01933 651024).

After Irthlingborough Lock, where the Nene Way rejoins the river from Irthlingborough, to run along the left bank, the Nene generally curves anti-clockwise, round the spur of the hills, to Upper and Lower Ringstead locks.

After the Association of Youth Clubs' Camp, there is a track leading to the Irthlingborough–Little Addington road. The river channel passes a lake on the right as it gently curves northeast, being crossed by a pipe bridge and then by a footbridge, and flanked on the right bank by a series of lakes, once again left as a result of former gravel workings, and the settlements of Stanwick, where a Roman villa, one of a number built along the Nene Valley, once stood and Raunds, the 'home' of the British army boot. At this footbridge, the Nene Way turns once again away from the river to proceed northwest to Little Addington (St Mary's church dating from the thirteenth century, telephone at the Bell public house ☎ 01933 651700), one mile away. There are a number of stone and thatched cottages in this picturesque village and, during World War II, a large number of Italian prisoners of war were lodged there.

On the right bank here is the site of the now deserted Mallows Cotton village which, together with its neighbours at West and Mill Cotton were abandoned following the Black Death and changes in agricultural practices. The remains of the villages can still be seen as lumps and bumps in the ground.

There is a weired side channel on the left and a further side channel on the right bank. After passing a lake on the left bank, the Nene's course is straighter, towards the north as it approaches Upper Ringstead Lock, some 2½ miles from Irthlingborough Lock. Here the Nene Way, leading from Little Addington, crosses the river in its track towards Ringstead village and a footpath leads across the field to Great Addington. There is a sluice and footbridge here at the lock, where the winding wheel has been replaced and, just before this, a further side channel to the right.

The name 'Ringstead' means circular place and the village itself lies one mile to the right of the lock. The shape of the parish suggests that it was once part of the parish of Raunds. Ringstead has a post office, a fish and chip shop and St Mary's church, which has a thirteenth-century west tower. Gravel extraction at Kinewell Lake to the west of the village, revealed an iron age hut circle some 11 yards in diameter. The remains of a Roman villa were also found and excavations uncovered a tessellated floor as well as many Roman and Iron Age artefacts. The deserted village of Mill Cotton, lies to the west of the parish. The nearby Ringstead Grange Trout Fishery, opened in 1980, offers fishermen 36 acres of water in which to fish for trout and salmon.

Just after Upper Ringstead Lock, both the minor channels on the left and right banks rejoin the main channel. The Nene meanders to the northeast, passing the last in the series of lakes on both banks which have shadowed the Nene since Irthlingborough. A marina development is being undertaken here at Blackthorn Lake and a further backwater is present on the left bank, leading to a mill, adjacent to the old railway viaduct crossing. This mill is known as Willy Watt Mill. It was mentioned in the Domesday Book and, over the years, has been used for cloth processing, corn grinding, paper making and grinding bones for use as phosphates in agriculture. The water wheels still remain today.

There was once a second mill at this location but it was demolished when the railway was built.

Shortly after the junction with the mill channel and just over half a mile from its neighbour is Lower Ringstead Lock, where the road from the mill to Ringstead crosses the river. Here is located the Willy Watt Marina (☎ 01933 622038 or 07710 094081 fax 01933 462470), where there is a water point and pump-out within the marina (charges apply), moorings, a slipway and dry dock owned by the marina. There was apparently no person named 'Willy Watt' after whom the site was named but instead the name seems to be a corruption of 'Willow Islands', the name by which this location was known in the fifteenth century. There is no telephone at the lock, the nearest public telephone being at Great Addington. Roads lead both to this village and to Ringstead itself from the lock but both are a long walk away. Close to the lock there is good access to the river for canoes. The Nene Way leaves the river again at Mill Road in the direction of Woodford village although a footpath continues along the right bank of the river as it passes Kinewell Lake on the right bank and smaller lakes on the left bank, before bending to the west. Boaters proceeding upstream are warned here to keep to the left.

This spot is known locally as 'Ringstead shallows' but more widely as the Mid Northants fishery and record carp have been caught here. Kinewell Lake is named after an ancient spring and is now a pocket park nature reserve, consisting of 50 acres of flooded gravel pits and 86 acres of adjoining meadows. The pits are connected to the Nene, which enables fish to migrate between the two water bodies. Insect life is particularly abundant here and the reserve is a haven for migratory birds.

The Nene then spends the next two and a half miles winding around its valley, through a broad expanse of meadows and the very pleasant scenery may be taken slowly and enjoyed. At the point of the first bend, the footpath on the right bank moves away to Ringstead and the Nene passes under the old railway bridge, just after which a minor tributary joins on the left and past Woodford Riverside where there were visitors' moorings in addition to other facilities but which now appear to have closed down. The Nene then continues its course, curling northwest past Woodford village.

Woodford

Woodford is a large village, inhabited since Saxon times, and appears in the Domesday Book as Wodeford, meaning ford by a wood. There are moorings just before the church on the left bank, although these seem solely to be private moorings. In the church itself, St Mary the Virgin, a mummified human heart was found in 1867. Many believe this to be the heart of Sir Walter Traily, the lord of the manor, who died on Crusade in 1290. There are oak effigies of Sir Walter and of his wife, Eleanor, in the north aisle. However, an alternative version tells that this is the heart of Roger de Kirketon, also a lord of the manor, who died in Norfolk in 1280. In 1964 a photograph of the altar of the church showed the ghostly figure of a knight, kneeling at the altar, but whether it was of Sir Walter or Roger de Kirketon or whether an alternative 'more rational' explanation exists are matters of conjecture.

Like many churches on this reach, the spire of St Mary the Virgin overlooks the valley from its proud position on the hill. The church is now on the edge of the village but there is evidence that this was not always so. The grassy bumps, in a nearby field, reveal the outlines of houses. Perhaps they were deserted after the Black Death or, possibly, they simply fell into disuse because of the changing fortunes of the manor?

Woodford also contains Woodford House, owned in the first half of the nineteenth century by a friend of the Duke of Wellington and often frequented by the Duke himself. Later, General Charles Arbuthnot, when living in the house in the late 1850s, started the Woodford Iron Ore Company, mining from an adit in the grounds of the house. The enterprise was considerably helped by the opening of the Kettering to Cambridge railway link in 1865.

The village boasts a stores, post office, fish and chip shop and a number of pubs where food is obtainable, the Prince of Wales (☎ 01832 735431), the Dukes Head (☎ 01832 732224) and the White Horse (☎ 01832 732646). There is also a public telephone in the village centre. Woodford now contains modern villas and is not otherwise interesting architecturally. It does however, contain other interesting features. The Three Hills Barrow is a burial ground which may date to the Neolithic or Bronze Age, and is to be found in Three Hills Field. On the outskirts of the village, towards Denford is Woodford Shrubbery (also known as Stone Pit Common), an area rich in wild flowers, insects and butterflies. The Shrubbery is reputedly the place where, in former times, limestone workers gathered for illicit drinking sessions. Near to the Shrubbery are the terraced remains of Lord St John's Dower House, demolished in the early nineteenth century.

In addition, from the vantage point of the old post mill site to the north of the village, ten church spires may be viewed.

The Nene continues east, past a weired side channel on the right bank, which rejoins the main channel by the old railway bridge downstream of Woodford Lock. The river then turns to the north and back east as it approaches the lock. A footpath from Woodford about a mile away, runs close to the left bank and then the left bank of the side channel, while the Nene Way rejoins the left bank of the main channel just upstream of the lock, having travelled through Woodford village. Woodford Lock is still accompanied by its neighbour, the old water mill.

After passing through Woodford Lock, the navigator enters a spacious broad reach, for the next mile to Denford. Shortly after the lock, a footpath moves away on the left bank towards Woodford Grange and the road to Islip. The Nene Way does not follow the serpentine windings of the Nene here but continues to pursue a straight course due east to Denford Lock. A minor footpath does however, continue to follow the left bank as the river curls south, east and then northeast back over the former railway line (with a warning sign to keep left when travelling downstream) before splitting into two upstream of Denford Lock where the former wooden blocks on the guillotine gate have been replaced with metal. The minor channel moves towards the village of Denford and often contains Aylesbury ducks, hoping for titbits from passers by. In summer the channel can be a mass of water lilies and the adjacent pollarded willows are also a feature. 'Denford' could mean settlement on a hill slope but was recorded in Domesday as 'Deneford', with the more likely meaning of 'ford in a valley'. The parish contains evidence of the former ridge and furrow agriculture, while a mound at the south of the village is all that remains of a former windmill. Denford church, Holy Trinity, which dates mainly from the thirteenth century, rises majestically above the trees while the churchyard contains a Northamptonshire Wildlife Trust reserve, a one-acre site of grasslands, ponds and springs, with mossy lichened walls. The reserve is home to caterpillars, butterflies, ash, hawthorn, willow, wild flowers and abundant birdlife.

Denford village itself is a mixture of stone and brick built houses but most of the former thatched roofs have been replaced by slates and tiles. The village has a telephone and postbox and the Cock Inn (☎ 01832 735565) where Indian food may be obtained. The minor channel passes the outskirts of the village and then curls north to flow parallel to the main channel and run between it and the Denford to Thrapston road, rejoining the main channel just downstream of the A14 road bridge. The main Nene continues northeast. Private moorings are available on both sides of the channel upstream of Denford Lock, and the only formal public moorings were those just downstream at Thrapston Mill Marina, which has now been closed. The stretch from here to Thrapston sees the river loop past pleasant marshy meadows, with a number of small streams crossing the flood meadows to join with the Nene.

A small backwater on the right bank flows immediately around the lock and a farm bridge crosses the channel on the approach to the lock. At this bridge, the Nene Way turns away from the Nene to head north towards the A14, which crosses the Nene at its new bridge. Close by is the viaduct for the now dismantled railway at which use of the higher arch is recommended. There is an adjoining caravan, camping and picnic site on the left bank. From here, it is a short walk to Thrapston.

Thrapston

Thrapston has a full range of facilities and a market on Tuesday, although many of the shops still close early on Thursdays. It has been a market town since King John granted it a charter in 1205 and once boasted two railway stations, neither of which now survives. It lies on the edge of the historic and once much larger Rockingham Forest, an area itself of much historical and nature interest.

On the west wall of the thirteenth-century St James' church is a tablet, depicting the stars and stripes, the crest of Sir John Washington, a former lord of the manor of Thrapston. This Washington died in 1668 but was the ancestor of the more famous Washington – George and the family crest formed the basis for the flag of the United States of America, a century later.

Thrapston Bridge, a nine-arched mediaeval bridge, divides Thrapston from its neighbour Islip, although the original structure has been widened and five arches of the bridge were rebuilt, following the serious flood of 1795. It is however, offset and small and the current can be tricky. Care should therefore be taken when navigating it. Opposite the bridge now is a picnic site for boaters and walkers and Environment Agency short stay (48 hour) moorings and a water point has been installed at the bridge moorings, under a joint initiative by the Environment Agency and Anglian Water. The Agency are also considering the installation of a pump-out close to the bridge. There is a choice of refreshment facilities at the bridge ends. On the Thrapston side the Bridge Hotel (☎ 01832 732128) offers food and accommodation as does the Woolpack (☎ 01832 732578) on the Islip bank. In the nineteenth century barges came frequently to Thrapston and the old wharves stand as a memory. A major new development by Charles Church is taking place on the Thrapston side of the bridge.

This bridge also marks the approximate location where the pronunciation of the river changes. From its source, it has so far been the 'Nen'. Now, downstream to its outfall, it is the 'Neen'.

Islip

Islip, whose name derives from an old English word meaning 'slippery place', referring to the hill leading down to the Nene banks, has Islip House, once the home of Thomas Squire, one of the leaders of the bid to make the Nene navigable between Thrapston and Peterborough in 1737. A secret passage leads from the house to the Woolpack Inn. The Washington connection can also be seen in Islip Church, St Nicholas, which contains a memorial tablet to Mary Washington. Near here was the factory of the Loveday family, of which eight generations harvested bulrushes, to be made into mats, baskets, horse collars and chair seats. The factory eventually closed in 1960.

There is a pipe crossing, just upstream of the bridge and the Nene Way follows the road through Islip, moving away from the river at this point.

Just downstream of the bridge is a broad reach, where in summer water lilies proliferate, as do the private moorings for the riverside properties. A track leads from Islip to Islip Mill and Lock. The mill in former times stood close to wharfs and warehouses and, until 1960, corn was ground there. Below the mill is Thrapston Lagoon, one of the biggest gravel pits in the country, adjoining the high ridge along the road from Aldwincle to Lowick. It contains an old wildfowl decoy and is just the largest example of the proliferation of gravel workings in this area. It is also the home of the Middle Nene (Thrapston) Sailing Club (☎ 01832 732871) whose moorings are on the right bank, ¼ mile downstream of the lock. There are 48-hour public moorings downstream of the lock on the right bank and the Agency are considering extending this facility.

There is a weired side channel on the right bank, with the mill race on the left bank, while the main channel continues as the middle channel to the lock where the guillotine gate is now electrically powered. Here the Nene Way rejoins the left bank of the river and a track continues for a little way along the right bank. Downstream, the mill race rejoins the main channel.

Islip to Wadenhoe

In the winter the meadows (around Titchmarsh Mill) flooded and my grand parents had to move upstairs in the Mill and abandon the lower rooms to the water

Mrs Julyans

In this stretch the maximum headroom at average summer water level is 7'3" (2·2m).

After leaving Islip, the scenery changes to a succession of flat more featureless meadows, forming the flood plain of the river. The Nene curls under three footbridges in quick succession. These are low and care should be taken. The river then moves to the northeast. Generally, the navigation is however, better on this stretch than downstream of Titchmarsh. The Nene Way then again moves away from the river to follow the right bank of another of the river's major tributaries, Harper's Brook, which rises close to Corby, near Desborough. The Nene Way continues along the bank, passing the lakes on both sides of the brook and of the main channel forming Titchmarsh Nature Reserve. This reserve, lying close to the A605 and Aldwincle village provides superb bird watching facilities and consists of 200 acres of former gravel pits, wetland meadows and a large heronry, comprising the Titchmarsh Duck Decoy, built by Lord Lilford in 1885. It is now managed by the Northamptonshire Wildlife Trust. The reserve is also well known for great-crested grebe, mallard and sand martins and incorporates a right of way along the adjacent former railway line.

An overhead power line crosses the river at this point and the succession of lakes continues until Brancey Bridge on the Aldwincle – Thorpe Waterville road is reached. Brancey Brook also provides a fluvial border to the reserve.

Gravel extraction in this area revealed the wooden remains of a Roman bridge and causeway across the river. This was part of the old Gartree road, linking Leicester and Godmanchester.

Immediately by the reserve, there is a minor backwater to the right as the main Nene turns north. After a further half mile, Titchmarsh Bridge crosses, carrying a track to meet the A605 and the road to Titchmarsh and Brancey Brook moves off from the left bank to join Harpers Brook, just before one of the latter's two junctions with the Nene. The old bridge has now been removed and the Environment Agency are in the process of constructing a new bridge to give a 3m air draught at normal water level. The Nene Way here moves off from Harpers Brook, in the direction of Aldwincle to the west to rejoin the left bank of the Nene close to Wadenhoe. The river then turns slightly west to pass the marina at Titchmarsh Mill (☎ 01832 720380) where there are the headquarters and moorings of the Middle Nene Cruising Club, adjacent to Titchmarsh Lock. There is a slipway here for members' use only and the village of Thorpe Waterville is accessible but only after a mile walk from the lock, along a track to the A605, across which a footpath also leads to Titchmarsh.

There is a telephone box on the main road and a postbox nearby. Environment Agency short term moorings are available on the left bank just downstream of the lock. The Agency had installed solar panels at Titchmarsh to provide an environmentally friendly power source and lock operation but following the theft of the panels, the guillotine door is electrically powered by means of a generator.

The Nene meanders in a generally northeasterly direction passing the end of the Nature Reserve, before meeting the bridge crossing of the Thorpe Waterville-Aldwincle road.

Aldwincle

The name 'Aldwincle' probably originates from a bend in the river. In the Domesday Book, it is shown as 'Eldewincle' from the Saxon 'wincel' meaning 'bend or corner'. The village has a church at either end and John Dryden, the poet and playwright, was born in the rectory of All Saints Church in 1631. The church is now disused but the rectory stands, as a thatched house, opposite. St Peter's church is however, still in use and is interesting for the remains of fourteenth century glass figures of St George and St Christopher in the south windows.

Afternoon tea is available at times at Pear Tree Farm tea rooms and, Aldwincle still has a post office/stores, telephone box by the village hall and a postbox by the village sign.

Thorpe Waterville

The Nene passes close to Thorpe Waterville at this point and its character is narrow and winding as it approaches the early-fourteenth-century bridge in the village. Thorpe Waterville does have the remains of a Norman castle, in respect of which a licence to crenellate was given to the Bishop of Lichfield in 1301 and, on the left of this, across a meadow, stands a farmhouse, all that now remains of the mansion house of the Waterville family, although signs of the moat are still present. There is a postbox 100 yards after Thorpe Cottage on the left hand side and a public telephone box in the village. Meals and refreshments are available at the Fox public house (☎ 01832 720274).

Having passed Thorpe Waterville, the Nene loops west and after a further half mile, meets the second outfall of Harper's Brook/Brancey Brook on the left bank. There are alder woods on the bank here and the river departs from its previous narrow sinuous course to become broad and deep, dividing round a small wooded island. The navigation channel is to the left but the backwater is popular with fishermen and crammed with tench.

Beyond this island, on the right bank is Achurch (Wadenhoe) Meadow. This SSSI is a flower meadow, containing over 100 different species of flowering plant and the former course of the Nene can be seen across the meadows, which also provide suitable breeding and feeding grounds for birds, such as redshank, snipe and lapwing. On the left bank, opposite, a ridge of limestone descends to the river, the ridge covered by old alderwood, a species once very common along the Nene and pollarded willows. Several brooks arise within the meadows.

Wadenhoe

Having passed Aldwincle on the left bank, the Nene curls back north again and the Nene Way joins the left bank from Aldwincle, close to a wooded area just upstream of Wadenhoe. There is a weired backwater on the right bank, while the main channel passes the isolated church of St Michael and All Angels on the left bank. This backwater joins another side channel going around Wadenhoe Lock where the guillotine gate is electrified. The main channel flows past Wadenhoe village. The name 'Wadenhoe' is probably derived from the Saxon for 'Wada's spur of land'. It has a bridge dating from 1760, with three round arches and an attractive long village street. The remains of a Neolithic mortuary enclosure and two Bronze Age round barrows have been found. The church of St Michael and All Angels is situated on a high hill slightly removed from the village. It contains sixteenth and seventeenth-century box tombs and a bell tower with a saddleback roof. The bells here are said to produce the most musical peal in the county. There are also interesting head corbels on the chancel arch, one representing a green man, and one a man with toothache. When entering the church, visitors are reminded to be careful to remember that there are two or three steps down to it, by the tale of a Mrs Mayes of Aldwincle. This lady was said to have been late for the harvest festival on one occasion, to have fallen down the steps and to have hit her head on the floor. The stain at the bottom of the stairs is said to be her blood, which soaked into the floor, before it could be cleaned up! The church also contains a memorial tablet to the former squire, Thomas Hunt and his bride Caroline, who were robbed and killed by bandits near Salerno in Italy, while on honeymoon in 1824. The estate was afterwards inherited by George Ward Hunt, who became Chancellor of the Exchequer in the Disraeli government, with the result that Wadenhoe was the first village to have a postal telegraph office to help him keep in touch. When leaving the church, a look down the hill towards the river is recommended, where what is now a landlocked oxbow, once part of the original channel, can still be seen.

When going up the hill to the church, a number of strange humps and bumps will be noticed. These are possibly, the earthworks of a long forgotten castle or of the original village, abandoned after the plague, although some say that they are simply the result of a landslide. The old mill over the hill from the Church on the northeast side of the village, has a roof tiled in Collyweston tiles. Near the mill is a circular dovecote, built in 1650, which is a county heritage site and the interior of which is well worth viewing. The Nene Way passes the mill.

The village can present a very pleasant picture, particularly in the summer months, when cream teas are served at the village hall. Close to the Kings Head pub (☎ 01832 720024) there is often a collection of caravans and many cottages are thatched and constructed of local stone. While there are moorings at the Kings Head for patrons of the pub, there are no 'stand alone' public moorings in the village and the IWA have asked the Environment Agency to consider installing such moorings. A water point has been installed adjacent to the Kings Head, as a co-operative venture between the Environment Agency and Anglian Water. The village has a conference and training centre in Wadenhoe House (☎ 01832 720777), a telephone box and a postbox on the Aldwincle road, through the village, which is within easy distance of the lock and the moorings that adjoin it. There is good canoe access and the Nene Way can be followed through Wadenhoe as it moves away from the Nene, to follow the road into the village. After the moorings at the Kings Head, the mill channel leads off the left bank to the mill just upstream of the lock.

Wadenhoe to Oundle

Sauntering at east, I often love to lean o'er old bridge walls and mark the flood below whose ripples through the weeds of oily green like happy travellers, mutter as they go
John Clare

The stretch of the Nene between Wadenhoe and Oundle has a headroom, at average summer water levels, of 7'3" (2·3m).

The lock at Wadenhoe, which has an electrically powered guillotine gate, leads into a deep wide pool and the village, the lock and their settings still convey something of the feel of a settlement in the wilderness. Downstream of the village, the 'lynch' escarpment is thick with trees, while to the west is a wild wooded track, once part of Rockingham Forest. It is the remains of a once great wood named 'Bareshanks', said

itself to be named after the dilapidated appearance of Black Watch deserters, caught there in 1743.

After Wadenhoe Lock, the next stretch to Lilford takes the voyager past boathouses, the channel being flanked with water meadows. After the lock, the back channel from the right rejoins the main channel, while the Nene Way, having followed the road to the mill through Wadenhoe then turns to the west and crosses the left-hand side channel and the main channel ¼ mile after the lock, before dividing into two just to the west of Achurch. The main Nene Way moves off to the north through the very pleasant wooded lynches. It tracks northeast through the lynches, before rejoining the Nene, adjoining Lilford Park, for a short distance by the B662 road.

The southern branch becomes an 'ordinary footpath' and continues to Achurch and the Achurch to Thorpe Waterville road. Achurch has been settled since the Iron Age and is named after the Saxon 'Aas-Kirk', 'the church by the water'. In Achurch is a well, a memorial to Thomas Powys, whose grandson became the first Lord Lilford. William Peake, born in Achurch in 1603 became Lord Mayor of London while Alfred Leete, born there in 1882, was the artist responsible for the famous 'Your Country needs you' recruiting poster of the First World War.

A footpath incorporating the Nene Way leads from the Church, St John the Baptist, built in 1218, to the river, flanked by grazing meadows on both sides. About 1830, the village was however, rebuilt by Lord Lilford, who demolished the former houses and replaced them with estate houses; lumps and bumps in the field on the other side of the road are all that remain of the former village.

The church has Saxon origins but was rebuilt at the end of the thirteenth century in the shape of a cross, by Sir Asceline de Waterville, in gratitude for a safe delivery from the crusades. Sir Asceline's tomb is in the church. There is a telephone box and postbox on the road through Achurch, which can be reached from the Nene via the footpath through the churchyard.

The Nene turns to the northwest and the left side channel rejoins a quarter of a mile further downstream. A private footbridge crosses and after a short distance, the Nene Way joins on the right bank. A weired side channel joins on the left, just upstream of Lilford Lock and runs parallel to the main channel for a short distance, before rejoining it.

Lilford

Lilford Lock, with its 'haunted look', is about a mile from Wadenhoe Lock and one of the most beautiful spots along the navigation. Its guillotine gate is also now electrically powered. The nearby graceful humpbacked balustraded stone bridge, carrying the road to Pilton has few equals in the country. It is set amongst the lynch escarpments, in the midst of the Nene valley, amidst woods and spinneys. The Nene flows directly by Lilford Hall, a Jacobean mansion built around 1635 of Ketton stone and noted for its unique double chimney stacks and superb façade. It is not open to the public but may be seen through the trees. Lilford was previously a Saxon village, but the first Lord Lilford demolished this in 1755 when the hall grounds were landscaped to create a 240-acre parkland estate, centred on the house. The church survived until 1788 when it was dismantled and partly re-erected as a folly in Achurch churchyard. The Nene here did not always have the attributes in keeping with such grandeur, however, for it was described by the fourth Baron Lilford, in the mid nineteenth century, as a deep, slow moving, muddy, weak stream. This Lord Lilford was the most famous inhabitant of the hall. He was a celebrated ornithologist who introduced the little owl into Britain and created aviaries within the estate between 1860–90. He is also remembered as the author of *The Birds of Northamptonshire*. The fact that the Nene was a slow moving, weak stream at that point is supported by the events of the winter of 1889, when, with the river completely frozen over, Lord Lilford organised an ox roast on the ice. On his death in 1896 he was buried in Achurch churchyard.

There is a public telephone close to the lock at Pilton, some quarter of a mile away on the left bank, with a postbox near the crossroads. The Nene Way moves off from the river to follow the B662 road southeast at the stone bridge by the lock and to track through Wigsthorpe (where there is also a public telephone box to the east of the village) and Barnwell, on its route back to the river.

The Nene continues past Lilford Park which is now no longer open to the public and then flows north past Lilford Lodge Farm. At the same time, Pilton vicarage and church, St Mary and All Saints appear on the left bank which form a fine group with the old manor house.

Between Pilton and Barnwell, the Nene travels sinuously through an almost unspoilt valley setting with high ground either side typified by water meadows with cattle grazing. A backwater from Stoke Doyle village joins on the left bank. As the river moves northwest, a footpath leading from Lilford joins the right bank and meets the Oundle to Barnwell road along which the Nene Way has travelled on its journey back towards the Nene. After a further ¼ mile, the river reaches a weired side channel on the left on the approach to Upper Barnwell Lock some two miles from Lilford. A second side channel leaves on the left immediately upstream of the lock, skirts round the south, west and north of the lakes in Barnwell Country Park and joins the first side channel at two points either side of the Barnwell–Oundle road. The main channel continues to Upper Barnwell Lock where there is a water point. Upper Barnwell Lock now has an electrically powered guillotine gate. Adjacent to the lock on the left bank is Barnwell Mill (☎ 01832 273726) now a restaurant and bar but with a long history. The mill is probably the oldest on the river, for while the present building is just over 300 years old, there has been a mill on the site since at least AD875 when a mill is referred to in the Anglo Saxon Chronicle. The mill has a public telephone when open, but the nearest public box is on the road to Oundle. Turn left, round the church and left again along the A427 past a garage. Barnwell village to the southeast has a post office/stores and the Montagu Arms pub (☎ 01832 273726), named after the village's most famous family, the Montagus. This is a fine old building, in a pleasant setting, approached over an old stone bridge. Montagu is the family name of the Earls of Sandwich and many Montagus are commemorated in the ruined All Saints church, which was partly demolished in 1825. Today, only the thirteenth-century St Andrews remains for worship. The chancel of this church was remodelled by Sir Gilbert Scott in 1851 but fifteenth-century stained glass windows have been retained. Additionally, among the carved flowers and leaves that decorate the north doorway is a face with a tongue sticking out. This is the mediaeval 'Jack in the Green' said to relate to an old May Day custom when young men camouflaged themselves with leaves when flirting with young girls. To the southeast of the church, are the Lathams Almshouses, built in 1601. The gardens of Barnwell Manor which can be reached via a beech lined footpath over the stone bridge from the church, include the ruins of a thirteenth-century castle, said to be haunted by the ghost of a monk with a whip. It was built around 1266 by Berengar Le Moyne, and was possibly, the first in the country to be built in the monumental style. At the time of the dissolution of the monasteries, the castle was bought from Peterborough Abbey by Sir Edward Montagu, who built a new house in the outer courtyard. On a less prosaic scale, the grounds also contain the remains of a Nissen hut This is a reminder of the commandeering of the Manor House during the Second World War, when it was used as a field hospital for the United States forces. Now the estate is back in private ownership and is being restored. The Nene at this point seems unsure of its passage towards Oundle, first approaching the town, and then veering away through flood meadows through Oundle Marina and old flooded gravel pits – before looping onwards to Polebrook and Ashton.

Oundle

Just after the Upper Barnwell lock, is Barnwell Country Park. This site, an oasis of calm between the Nene and a backwater comprises 37 acres of former gravel pits, lakes, reed beds and grassland and is the home to the largest colony of noctule bats in the United Kingdom as well as a large number of newts. It also contains a children's activity area and a boules court as well as a wildlife garden. The park has good access for the disabled and it and its visitor centre are open all year round (☎ 01832 273435). The stretch of the Nene by the park has good canoe access. Adjoining the park is Oundle Mill (☎ 01832 272621, www.oundlemill.com), due to open in March 2007, advertised as having casual and formal restaurants, bedrooms, meeting rooms and disabled access. There will be a limited number of moorings for patrons in the mill pond. Immediately after the lock, the Oundle to Barnwell road crosses the Nene. The bridge is however low and askew and care should be taken in navigating it. Just downstream of Upper Barnwell Lock are the headquarters of the Oundle Cruising Club, on the left bank, which are open at weekends in season and just downstream of this is the entrance to Oundle Marina (☎ 01832 272762), although great care is required

when entering the channel from upstream. The marina is a secure site at night and contains a car park, chandlery, a slipway, a water point, refuse disposal, workshop facilities, craneage, fuel, toilets and showers and both temporary and long stay moorings. Here also are based Fairline Boats Ltd. St Peter's church spire, a prominent Oundle landmark, is clearly visible from the marina.

The Nene Way moves to the east, through Oundle Marina to cross the Nene at Lower Barnwell Lock and the side channel, as it rejoins the main channel just downstream of the lock and continues along the left bank.

Downstream of Oundle Marina and 1½ miles from its neighbour, stands Lower Barnwell Lock where the guillotine gate is now electrically powered and immediately afterwards the two side channels rejoin the main Nene which flows again as one. A footpath leads over these backwaters and across the meadows up Basset Farm Road to Oundle, emerging at the Market Place. The Nene turns southeast, with poplars prominent on the south bank and the silver spire of Achurch church can still be seen beyond Lilford Woods.

The river then turns south and after ¼ mile is crossed by the A605 adjacent to which are private moorings. A semi-circular backwater joins immediately downstream. The Nene Way diverts round this, then returns to follow the left bank. There is a densely wooded area on the right bank leading up from the Barnwell–Armston road and, after this area, the river turns northeast and, after a further ¼ mile, north. For the last 2–3 miles the Nene has skirted the town of Oundle ending up encircling it, but this is an unfair course, for Oundle is well worth a visit. Oundle has been a settlement since the Iron Age and the name 'Oundle' comes from 'Un dalum', a 'dal' being a share of land and 'undals' either people dispossessed of land or who took over land not given to others. There was once a monastery here dedicated to St Wilfred, who died in AD709. The north bridge of the town was destroyed in a flood in 1570, but was rebuilt the following year and widened just prior to First World War, to accommodate the increase in traffic. It now looks out, on the western side, over its stone parapet on Oundle Wharf, a short canal, about 400 yards long, dug from the Nene just downstream of what is now the A427 road bridge, when the local brewery built maltings on the edge of town. It is now very popular with anglers. The town contains many fine seventeenth and eighteenth-century buildings and has been greatly helped by the diversion away of the A605, Peterborough to Northampton Road in the mid 1980s. The diverted route follows the course of the old railway line.

Perhaps the finest of the buildings of Oundle is the Talbot Hotel (☎ 01832 273621) whose 400-year old grey stone front was constructed in the early seventeenth century by William Whitwell, whose initials, with the date 1626, appear in the gable of a nearby house. Whitwell used materials from Fotheringhay Castle in this construction and the staircase within the hotel is said to be the one walked down by Mary, Queen of Scots, on the way to her execution. Around the market place in particular, are a number of fine old buildings, including Bramston House, which dates from the eighteenth century, the former White Horse Inn from 1641 and Lathams Hospital which is thirty years older still.

At the rear of the Talbot is Drummingwell Lane, so called because it was said that a ghostly drumming came from the well behind the hotel, when an important event was to take place. The well has however, now been filled in.

St Peter's Church spire, at 208 feet high, is a landmark for many miles around and it was famously climbed by one Bailey in 1880.

Oundle also possesses a famous public school, which had its origins, in the fourteenth century, as a small grammar school, attached to the Guild of Our Lady of Oundle. After the dissolution of the monasteries, a famous former pupil, Sir William Laxton, rescued the school and his foundation, in 1556 of the Old Laxton School, which was rebuilt in 1852, is sandwiched between the market place and the graveyard of St Peter's Church. However, it was the later buildings that made the school most famous, particularly under the guidance of Frederick Sanderson, a famous headmaster of the school in the late nineteenth century. The school is now scattered throughout the town and is Oundle's biggest employer, numbering Sir Peter Scott amongst its former pupils. Oundle has a full range of facilities, shops, chemists, doctors, dentists, hotels, pubs, cafes, restaurants etc. There is a public telephone and information centre in the market place, where a market is held on Thursdays. On Wednesdays, however, many of the shops close early. There is also Oundle Museum (☎ 01832 272741) on the outskirts

of town, with exhibits tracing the history of the settlement over the past 2,000 years. There are at present no public moorings serving the town itself, although the creation of 120m of short stay moorings by the Environment Agency, is under consideration.

Oundle to Wansford

The brook seemed purling sweeter by
As freshened from the cooling light
And on its breast the morning sky
Smiles beautiful and bright

John Clare

The stretch of the Nene below Oundle has a maximum headroom, at average summer water levels, of 6'9" (2·1m) and there is a width restriction at Fotheringhay of 12'10" (3·9m).

The river below Oundle is broader and, downstream of the town, flanked with rich flood meadows. It is also deeper now, from here up to the tidal sluice at Dog-in-a-Doublet.

About one quarter of a mile downstream of the old A605 to Oundle, Ashton Lock is reached. This lock is about 1 mile from Oundle Bridge, and stands secluded in beautiful meadow surroundings. Upstream of the lock is a small weired backwater on the left bank, which curves around the lock. Immediately upstream of the lock a side channel on the right bank turns north to Ashton Mill, and rejoins the main channel by a small cut 200 yards further on. There are quiet moorings available on the right bank of this side channel at the junction although any mooring here would appear private rather than free public moorings.

Next to Ashton Mill the adjacent Victorian power station has been restored as a crafts/bygones exhibit area but the former Mill House Tea Room is now closed as is the former Dragonfly Museum. The Nene Way approaches Ashton Lock along the left bank of the main channel. The lock stands close to the village church. To reach the village, head up the hill from the river. Cross the main Nene at the footbridge and then the side channel at its bridge, head straight and then turn right on the road to the village.

Ashton

Ashton village is owned by the Rothschild family and contains a village green, horse chestnut trees and thatched cottages. It has a chapel and school dated 1705, but is mainly of a more modern construction, although with an 'olde worlde' feel. In 1860, Baron Rothschild bought the parish and around 1900, his son Charles rebuilt the village in local stone and thatch. He also converted the mill to supply the village with piped water and electricity.

The village pub, the Chequered Skipper (☎ 01832 273494) is widely known. It is a pleasant thatched structure, with the green in front of it being frequented by peacocks, originally introduced to the estate by the Rothschilds. The pub is at the far end of the village and takes its name from a rare butterfly, Ashton being the last place at which it was recorded, before becoming extinct in England. Adjoining the pub are a public telephone and postbox and the Nene Way runs past it along the road, on its way from Barnwell. Ashton's main claim to fame is however, the World Conker Championships, which have been held in the village every year since 1965, on the morning of the second Sunday in October. It is also famous for its nature reserve, Ashton Wold, which contains many old oaks, 250-years old or more and a four-acre lake planted with both marginal and emergent vegetation to attract dragonflies. The wold was created by Charles Rothschild (1877–1923) a keen conservationist, who created the society for the Protection of Nature Reserves (now the Royal Society for Nature Conservation) in 1912 and set aside part of his Ashton Estate as a nature reserve.

After Ashton Lock, from which the spire of Oundle Church is clearly visible, the Nene Way turns north to run parallel to the river bordered by water meadows. It is crossed by the footbridge carrying the footpath running from Oundle to Ashton, at which point the Nene Way crosses the Nene and the millstream at the mill to go through Ashton in a northeasterly direction to the village of Warmington. The millstream rejoins the main channel on the right bank after Ashton Mill, as it continues north past the east side of Oundle. A footpath continues on the left bank as the river turns briefly northwest, northeast, north and then northwest again, before crossing the New Road Bridge of the A605. The A427 running from the A605 then crosses the Nene and the footpath follows this, crossing to run along the right bank. Immediately downstream of this is Oundle Sailing Club, located at Oundle Wharf. The Nene continues in a general northwesterly direction, past the Oundle sewage treatment works on the left bank before turning northeast, by a very pleasant

heavily wooded area of countryside on the left bank. A weired side channel on the right bank leads downstream of Cotterstock Lock, which now has an electrically powered guillotine gate. This side channel is followed 200 yards further downstream by a second side channel, which joins with the first to meet at Cotterstock Lock, some two miles downstream of Ashton.

Immediately upstream of the lock, Cotterstock Mill stream leaves on the left, leading to the mill, which has now been converted into a private house. The mill race exits on the left bank of the Nene, past Cotterstock Church.

Cotterstock

Cotterstock was once a Roman settlement and, over a thousand years later, the poet John Dryden often stayed at the Jacobean Cotterstock Hall, where he enjoyed the views of the church and river. The church, St Andrews, is of interest, a small but spacious building with ancient drawings of deer on the left-hand side of the porch. This is not that surprising. The present building dates from the twelfth century and is built on the site of an earlier structure. In the year 1100 it would have been situated deep in the ancient Rockingham Forest now much reduced in size. The village now contains no shop or public house, and the nearest public telephone is ¼ mile downstream of the lock, on the main street through the village, turning left at the road bridge. The Nene vista remains essentially rural, passing through meadows where sheep graze.

The river then turns northeast and is crossed after a short distance by Cotterstock Bridge carrying the road leading to the A605 and Tansor village where the footpath moves away from the river. The Nene's next movement is to the northwest and then due north as it passes Tansor. Tansor, like Cotterstock has no pub or shops but because it is relatively straight, the stretch of the Nene adjoining it is used by the rowers of Oundle School and their landing stage is situated here on the right bank. Caution should be exercised here, due to the possible presence of the school racers. There is a telephone in the village centre by the church at the junction of the road from Cotterstock and the church, St Mary's has a quaint square shape with its churchyard going right down to the river, where it is framed by a tree-lined left bank. The Nene itself contains reeds and a pool of water lilies. The carved choir stalls at St Mary's came from the east end of Fotheringhay church, when the latter was demolished.

After skirting Tansor, the Nene turns northwest. Downstream of Tansor, the north bank is very tree lined. A small backwater runs from and joins the left bank within a very short distance and a second weired backwater, leaving from the right bank then runs between two lakes, parallel to the main course of the Nene on that bank, as the river continues north west to Perio Lock, some two miles from the lock at Cotterstock. At Perio Lock, the Agency are trialling a new wheel system mechanism for easier lock operation. A second, minor channel, then divides from the main river and continues to Perio Mill, now converted to a private residence and then curls northeast, matching the direction of the main Nene here, which flows past the northwestern side of the western most of the lakes. They are flooded former gravel quarries. These lakes are known as the Bluebell Lakes, and can be reached from Perio Lock. Additional moorings now exist on this stretch of the river, being available through Blubell Fisheries (☎ 01832 226042). Perio is a mediaeval name whose origins are unclear. Its mill is small compared to Ashton and the millstream is artificially stocked with trout and an important fishery.

The downstream end of Perio Mill channel rejoins the Nene after a short distance on the left bank. When proceeding upstream at this point, you are advised to 'keep right'. Two minor tributaries, from the west then meet the left bank in quick succession before the backwater from the weir rejoins the main channel from the south. The main Nene continues to flow east past the northern side of the Bluebell Lakes to pass the village of Fotheringhay.

Fotheringhay

The name 'Fotheringhay' has three possible derivations. It could be from 'Frodinga', 'the island of Froda's people'; from 'forth here inga' 'the island of people following an army leader' or, most likely, from 'fodring-eg' 'foddering island'. The suffix 'hay' refers to the clearing in Rockingham Forest where deer were foddered in winter.

At Fotheringhay, an earth mound is now the only reminder of the castle, which was most famously the execution site of Mary, Queen of Scots. The castle mound is covered in thistles, a poignant reminder of Mary, who

was said to have planted them there during here imprisonment. She had been incarcerated at Fotheringhay following her abdication from the Scottish throne, in 1567, subsequent to her marriage to Bothwell and flight to England. Eventually however, she was seen as the figurehead for English Catholics, disillusioned with the Protestant Elizabeth I and went to her fate on 8th February 1587. The castle however, had almost 500 years of history, before Mary met her end. It was built around 1100 by Simon de St Lys, the first Earl of Northampton and Huntingdon and husband of Maud, the great niece of William the Conqueror. A second castle was built in the fourteenth century around 1377, by Edmund de Langley, first Duke of York and fifth son of Edward I and, by the time of Henry VIII, there was a 'castle fair and meatly strong with very good lodgings in it', defended by double ditches with a very ancient and strong keep covering 10 acres. King Richard III was also born at Fotheringhay castle. Today, however, little remains. Apart from the raised round, the line of the moat is still visible but otherwise only crumbling masonry and tangled bushes signify the history of the site. A permit from the farmer, on whose land the castle remains now are, is needed to visit.

The village church is St Mary and All Saints but since the choir was allowed to decay and was later demolished in 1573, the building has a top heavy appearance, being now about half its original size, with the surrounds dwarfed by the lantern tower and weathervane. The latter depicts the falcon, the badge of the House of York. Within the church is buried Edmund, Duke of York, founder of the church and college in 1441, the memorial to whom was raised at the personal command of Elizabeth I. The Falcon (☎ 01832 226254) is also the name given to the old Inn at the east end of Main Street. The buildings on the south side of the Main Street dated by W A Pontin to the reign of Edward I, have been transformed into cottages. Fotheringhay has public telephones and a good canoe access to the Nene at the road bridge on the left bank. This eighteenth century bridge is of the stone humpedback variety with beautifully proportioned arches. It is however, set low and the navigable arch offset, so navigators are advised, particularly when going downstream, to keep well to the left to get a straight run through the largest left-hand arch, as the current is also a significant factor. There are willows 75–100 yards after the bridge, overhanging the river and care should also be taken around these. Close to and just upstream of the bridge is a water point, installed as a joint venture between the Environment Agency and Anglian Water.

Once Fotheringhay has been left behind, the countryside changes dramatically in character, the previous rolling nature of the banks now replaced by flat meadows and houses built from local stone. Moorings are available on payment at Castle Farm Cottage and there is a guest house at Castle Farm (☎ 01832 226326).

The Nene passes the roadway to Warmington Grange and shortly afterwards, is crossed by the Fotheringhay–Tansor road. A small tributary joins on the left bank. The Nene then curves southeast, crossing the former railway line, and then turns northeast, passing a small backwater on the right bank, before splitting just upstream of Warmington village. Here, the main navigation channel turns east and northeast to Warmington Lock, 2½ miles from Perio Lock.

On this stretch are a number of willow pollards in the fields, a feature throughout parts of the Nene Valley. These are willows, whose tops have been cut off above cattle grazing height. Willows produce lots of shoots, which grow into poles and were traditionally harvested on 3–15 year cycles. However, many of the traditional uses of the pollarded material, basket making, hurdle fencing etc. have declined and now grants are given by various organisations to restore and maintain these trees and their impact on the landscape.

The minor channel turns south then, after a loop, northeast where it itself splits in two. On the southernmost of these channels, which runs close to the adjacent A605 at this point, is the Red Lion public house (☎ 01832 280362) and the Eaglethorpe Mill, with the moorings of Elton Boat Club headquarters, just upstream within the millstream. For details contact the club (secretary ☎ 01572 723552). There is a weir at the junction of the minor split which carries a footbridge.

The Nene Way, having tracked across country from Fotheringhay crosses the Nene and the two side channels at Warmington Lock, 2½ miles from Perio Lock on its way towards Warmington village. The walk takes you just past the Eaglethorpe Mill and, via an underpass, across the A605 road to Eaglethorpe, a settlement founded by Danish invaders. The village was however, depopulated in the sixteenth century, when the Proby family enlarged the grounds of Elton Hall. The watermill became redundant in 1880 and was finally closed in the 1890s (it has now been converted into the Fired Earth Home Design Studios). Near the mill is a dovecote, made from a wooden framework covered in mortar, which is listed as a scheduled ancient monument. It has nesting boxes for 800 birds. When the adjacent A605 was being constructed, a Beaker burial, of a man buried 3,000 years ago, was discovered.

Adjacent to Eaglethorpe and the A605, is Warmington village, and the footpath referred to above takes you into this settlement via Chapel Street, where the first turn right leads to the post office/stores. There is also a telephone box and a postbox opposite the Red Lion public house.

Warmington

Warmington means 'the farm of Wyrm's people' and the village is 2 miles on foot from Ashton but, because of the sweeping bends of the Nene, 6 miles away by river. The Romans were active here and built a road between the two villages, its remnants surviving as part of the Nene Way. Warmington later belonged to the Abbey of Peterborough and was very prosperous in mediaeval times. Its church, St Mary the Virgin, finished in 1290, is noted for its broach spire. There is good access for canoes at the mill and short stay moorings and a water point are available at the Elton boat club.

The two side channels rejoin the main channel as the Nene curves northwest past a heavily tree-lined right bank (Rowleys Wood), and more minor backwaters connect with the river as it flows past Elton Park, passing Elton Hall on the right bank. This was never a castle, but was defended. There has been a house on this site since the Norman Conquest, with the present house completed in 1666. It contains a number of Old Masters and the state coach used by the owners to attend Queen Victoria's Jubilee. The library includes a prayer book, containing the writing of King Henry VIII. Elton Hall has been the home of the Proby family for 380 years. The hall is open to the public on Thursdays and Saturdays. Refreshments are available at the hall at Blooms Tea Room (☎ 01832 280468). The author Kenneth Grahame, famous for *The*

Wind in the Willows, spent many summers at Elton Hall and indeed, one of the islands in the Nene opposite Elton Hall, between the river and its side channels, is known as 'Ratty Island'.

One of the other main tributaries of the Nene, Willow Brook having risen near Corby, joins from the east here in two channels, one connected via a weir which carries a footpath and the other joining downstream of Elton Lock and Mill. At this point the channel again splits in two for a short distance, with Elton Lock on the northern, left hand, channel. Elton Lock is 1½ miles from Warmington Lock and, like the locks at Yarwell and Wansford further downstream, Elton Lock can be awkward to navigate coming from upstream. The southern channel moves to the west close to Elton village. Just upstream of Elton Lock are the private moorings of the Elton Estate but these have size restrictions due to turning space available, although available for public hire. At Elton Lock the guillotine gate is now electrically powered and the balance beams have been lowered and strengthened.

At Elton, pleasant woods almost march down to the water's edge. Aromatic poplars are pronounced. The village lies up a steep hill with the main road at the top, and includes a well provisioned stores and post office.

Elton

Elton, whose name means 'princes' farm' was formerly a farming village, but is now a Peterborough 'dormitory' settlement, with typical housing estates. The village green still survives with the Crown Inn and Restaurant (☎ 01832 280232) adjoining. The centre is very pleasant with a number of thatched cottages and there are five Roman sites with a major Roman road which can still be traced through part of the parish, confirming the important part in daily life that the river has played at least since those times. The parish boundaries were laid out by Saxon settlers and two Saxon gravestones can still be seen on the north side of the church. Stocks Green still has a set of stocks, after which the location was named and adjoining the Green is a water mill referred to in Domesday although the present building, a three storey brick structure, dates from about 1840. The church All Saints, is pleasant, with a William Morris stained glass window. For those who enjoy a fish meal, the Old Dairy has now been converted into the Loch Fyne

Restaurant (☎ 01832 280298) and the Black Horse Inn on the main road (☎ 01832 280240) also provides refreshments.

The footpath from the lock leads to the village green and Middle Street where, in addition to the village stores and post office, there is a telephone box on the road to Nassington. The footpath follows the road through Elton to rejoin the Nene again at Elton Bridge close to the sewage treatment plant on the south bank by 'the island' a wooded area between the Nene and its backwater.

At Elton, the Nene leaves Northamptonshire and enters Cambridgeshire (now the Administrative district of the Greater Peterborough Unitary Authority) and the river marks the county boundary for the next four miles. The river here is shallow and gravel bottomed.

Between Elton and Wansford, there are no sheltering woods, just open spacious countryside, mainly comprising water meadows with attractive rushy banks, although areas of the banks are tree lined.

Just upstream of the sewage treatment works, Elton Road Bridge carrying the road from Nassington crosses the Nene and the footpath rejoins the right bank continuing for ½ mile before splitting, after crossing the river at the next footbridge, one section continuing to Nassington, where it is joined by the Nene Way from Fotheringhay while the other tracks along the left bank. After two more minor channels join, the Nene turns north and divides, the minor stream where the route of the former railway line from Oundle crosses the Nene, heading over a weir north to rejoin the main channel downstream of Yarwell Lock, a low structure with a guillotine gate, three miles from Elton Lock. Between Yarwell and Peterborough the Nene has a maximum headroom, at average summer water levels, of 7'9" (2·4m).

Nassington

Wilgar bridge, carrying the Nene Way, crosses the channel which then turns northeast to pass by the village of Nassington, (whose name means 'farm of the headland dwellers') while a side channel loops in the direction of the village. Here moorings formerly existed at the Queens Head pub, having closed it has recently reopened as a restaurant and the moorings have been reinstated (☎ 01780 784006) This side channel is shallow so navigators are advised to proceed slowly. The Romans built a village at Nassington due to the extensive mineral workings in the locality in those days. Nassington itself supplied ironstone, while quarries at nearby Yarwell produced limestone for building, clay for bricks and gravel for road building. The Nene itself, of course, formed the means of transport. Nassington Church, All Saints, has a Saxon nave and fourteenth century wall paintings, with the remains of a Saxon cross in the churchyard. In 1942, a Saxon cemetery was found here, which contained 65 bodies, along with grave goods.

The Prebendel House, (☎ 01780 782575) to the southwest of the church, dates from the early thirteenth century and its hall still possesses original doorways. It was the base of an official (the Prebendary) of the Diocese of Lincoln. It is possibly the oldest inhabited house in Northamptonshire and certainly the oldest manor house. It still retains gardens of the fourteenth century style, together with fishponds, a fifteenth-century dovecote and a tithe barn museum. To the north, is the manor house, dating from around 1500. There are also the remains of several prehistoric barrows in the vicinity.

Food and refreshments can be obtained at the Black Horse public house, (☎ 01780 782324) from which a footpath leads to Wilgar Bridge and the flood meadows and there is a post office/stores and a telephone box at the far end of the village on the Apelthorpe Road.

The side channel continues northeast to rejoin the main channel, which continues to Yarwell Lock, which is due to be electrically powered in late 2006, and Mill, with the mill stream then leaving on the left bank. The footpath previously on the right bank, curves away to Wansford to the northeast. The water meadows here are prolific with flowers in spring/summer. At the mill (☎ 01780 782247) were shower, toilet, water and pump-out facilities, in addition to moorings but these are now closed except for the new Agency water point upstream of the lock, with no public facilities, other than moorings being available. The moorings should be booked in advance and the proprietors request that any dogs are kept on the boat. The Environment Agency is endeavouring to arrange for alternative facilities to be provided nearby. At present under consideration are the provision of 48-hour moorings here and also steam boat moorings, in conjunction with the Nene Valley Railway, the proposal is to facilitate a steam narrow boat trip from the railway station at Stibbington to Yarwell. Close to the mill is a caravan and camping site with fishing lakes and a picnic area (☎ 01780 782344).

Yarwell

The Nene Way footpath crosses the bridge at the mill on its way to Yarwell village which lies about ½ mile from the Nene with fine views over the river. The clearance at the bridge is low 7' (2·13m) at summer water levels. The village possesses a post office/stores and a public telephone box. Meals and refreshments can be had at the Angel public house (☎ 01780 782582). At the village church of St Mary Magdelene, parts of the thirteenth-century chapel remain and between Yarwell and Wansford, at the side of the King's Cliffe Road, are Roman remains, a building, possibly a bailiff's house and a quarry. By the Nene at Yarwell are the remains of a wharf where a number of mills, including a paper mill, formerly operated. Paper was produced for newspapers, until an explosion in 1855 put an end to business.

The Nene swings east past a further series of lakes, before turning north and then northwest past Ship End Pits stone quarry to where the Yarwell Mill stream rejoins the main channel. The Nene then divides again on the approach to Wansford Lock one mile from Yarwell Lock. The western left-hand channel contains the lock, although remnants of the old lock, as a sluice, still remain in the eastern right-hand channel. The footpath follows the left bank of the lock channel for a short distance, before circling to join the Nene Way and move away from the immediate bank side, in the direction of Wansford village. The remnants of Old Sulehay Forest lie just on the western side of the Yarwell–Wansford road at this point. The lock itself is a vertical gate, electrically powered structure and navigators are advised to approach it with great care when travelling downstream, when there is a heavy flow in the river, and to beware of the side channel weir hazard. Close to the lock are toilets, although the Environment Agency are considering installing 48-hour moorings downstream of the lock. The best access to Wansford village is via the footpath on the right bank by Wansford Old Bridge. This bridge was originally built of wood, but was replaced with a stone structure in the mid-thirteenth century and later partly rebuilt, after flood damage in 1796. The bridge arches on the village side are irregular. The small round arch next to a wider one is dated 1795, the next three 1672–4 and the next seven, 1577. On the bridge is a marker, showing the county boundary between the old Huntingdonshire and Soke of Peterborough. Wansford in fact now boasts three road bridges, since the old bridge has now been joined by the two modern structures carrying the A1. The Great North Road used to pass through the centre of the village, across the graceful old bridge whose architecture merits favourable comparison with the modern structures. Now the old bridge takes the B671 over the Nene. There is also a railway bridge just upstream of Wansford, built in 1850.

Wansford

Wansford is also known as Wansford-in-England, the name deriving from the local tale of one Barnabee who, in the reign of George III, arrived in the parish fleeing from the plague. Because of his fear of the disease, he was afraid to sleep in local inns and so spent the night on top of a haystack in a meadow by the river. However, during the night, the river rose sharply due to a storm upstream and the haystack floated away down the Nene. Its journey was however, halted when it became wedged in the buttresses of the Old Bridge. Next morning, when Barnabee awoke, he asked where he was. On being told that he was in Wansford and being confused about just how far he had travelled, he replied 'What, Wansford in England?' The name has stuck.

The most well known establishment in Wansford is the Haycock Inn, (☎ 01780 782223), dating from 1670, with its five bay centre and two bay wings. Parts of it date to the thirteenth century and it was an inn known as 'the Swan' until the eighteenth century, when it was renamed to commemorate Barnabee's voyage. The Inn Sign now depicts Barnabee. Wansford was a very important port with significant cargoes being unloaded even 100 years ago. The Haycock itself once adjoined a bustling wharf as, for example, quarried limestone and timber from the remnants of Rockingham Forest were loaded there, while grain and coal from up river were the main items unloaded. However no trace of the previous industry can be seen. There appears to be an informal arrangement for moorings here, whereby boats pull in to land just on the Peterborough side of the old Wansford Bridge. This mooring facility is not however, formally dedicated to public use and strictly only available to patrons of the Haycock, on whose land the facility lies.

Wansford also contains other pubs, one called 'The Paper Mill' (☎ 01780 782328) which is also a restaurant, being the only reminder of a local bustling paper industry in the eighteenth and nineteenth centuries, with the mills being situated in the grounds of Stibbington House nearby. The Cross Keys (☎ 01780 782266) is also in the village. Wansford also contains shops, a post office close to the Haycock and public telephone facilities. The Nene in fact splits the village since, while the greater part of the settlement lies to the south of the river, the church, St Mary the Virgin, and its surroundings, are to the north. The church has Saxon windows on the west wall. There is a restaurant, 'Fiddlesticks' just down from the Haycock (☎ 01780 784111).

On the left bank is a footpath and here too is a small local nature reserve, some 8 acres of grassland, hedges and streams forming well-grazed pastures, rich in chalk-loving plants and invertebrates. It is under the jurisdiction of the Northants Wildlife Trust and open in Spring and Summer. It fits in well with the general nature of the tree-lined field banks at Wansford.

The two channels rejoin opposite Stibbington House and flow to Wansford. So far in our journey, the Nene has flowed generally northeast from Northampton. Now, for the final leg of its trip to the sea, it turns east.

Once Wansford Old Bridge and its adjoining informal mooring area have been passed, a footpath continues along the right bank, past the Haycock, under the old bridge, before opening up into a tree-lined meadow area. The Nene is then crossed by the A1 bridge adjacent to which is a picnic area and toilets. At this point, a worthwhile detour could be made just to the north to Sacrewell Farm and Country Centre (open 7 days a week 0930–1700) (☎ 01780 782254). Sacrewell Mill is a small stone estate water mill dating from 1755. It is a three storey building and has the miller's house attached. 'The Miller's Kitchen' is open for snacks and gifts and campers and caravanners are welcome. It is now part of the Sacrewell Farm and Visitors Centre. The mill stream forms the boundary between the parishes of Wansford and Thornhaugh and the site contains prehistoric circles and Neolithic implements. The name 'Sacrewell' probably comes from the spring rising in one of the fields. There are the remains of several Romano-British villas on the farm and of buildings used for grain dying and malting.

Downstream of Wansford, a footpath continues for a short distance on both banks, with that on the left bank being the Nene Way. The Nene passes Wansford Pumping Station, where much of its water is diverted to Anglian Water's Rutland Water reservoir.

A short detour of two miles to the west of Wansford lies Bedford Purlieus, a 46 acre fragment of the old Rockingham Forest now owned by the Northamptonshire Wildlife Trust.

Wansford to Peterborough

Where the gay river laughing as it goes
Plashes with easy wave, its flaggy sides
And to the calm of heart, a calmness shows
What pleasure there abides
John Clare

Having left Wansford behind, the Nene sweeps past a series of lakes on its right bank and the A47 trunk road, which runs close to the left bank at this point. The Nene then turns south and here the Nene Way moves away from the bank once again as the river passes Stibbington, to which a road leads from the bank.

Stibbington

Stibbington is the home of the Nene Valley Railway, which crosses the Nene at this point and runs from there to Peterborough, even though the station at Stibbington is known as Wansford Station. Navigators are advised to use the right-hand arch of the railway bridge. The railway was previously part of the old London to Birmingham railway, which opened on 17 September 1838, but originally bypassed Northampton, due to a ridge of high ground to the south of the town. However, following pressure from the inhabitants of Northampton, the Nene Valley line was opened between Blisworth and Peterborough, on 2 June 1845, despite the opposition of local landowners, such as Lord Lilford and Lord Fitzwilliam. Ironically, the building of the line created a huge demand for commercial traffic on the Nene, with thousands of tons of rails and sleepers being delivered by barge. This

upsurge was, of course, purely temporary as the railway took over and assisted in the decline of commercial river traffic. In turn however, the growth of road traffic saw the death knell of the railway and the very last train ran on 4 November 1972, as the line was axed, as a result of the cuts instigated by Dr Beeching. However, enthusiasts managed to preserve the last seven miles of track, which now provide a genteel reminder of a bygone age of travel. The railway provides a fifteen-minute journey to Peterborough (talking timetable ☎ 01780 784404, general enquiries 01780 784444). It is the home of Thomas the Tank Engine and there is a shop, café and railway museum. Opposite the station at Wansford is a riverside picnic area and there are moorings just upstream of the railway bridge.

At nearby Stibbington Boatyard, the home of P M Buckle Narrow Boats (☎ 01780 783144) where there are some private moorings available but now no pump-out or toilets. Next door is A C Outboards and, slow passage, past moored vessels, is urged. The church at Stibbington (St John the Baptist) is modern, although nearby Stibbington Hall dates from 1625 and in its grounds, as well as in the area locally, have been found pottery relics of Roman times, although even more prominent finds have been uncovered just downstream. The Nene, while following a meandering course, continues to follow mainly an easterly direction. The scenery has certainly changed now. From the valley bottom with its picturesque fall, the banks are now more uninteresting having left their trees behind and now flat water meadows and pastureland border the Nene.

Leaving the Nene Valley Railway on the left bank for a time, the Nene crosses under a power line before dividing just upstream of Water Newton Lock. The Nene Way, having cut across from Nassington village, following the route of a former railway line, now rejoins the river to follow the northern more minor channel while the Hereward Way long distance footpath now follows the left bank of the main channel. The minor channel rejoins the Nene downstream of Water Newton Lock.

Water Newton

The main Nene continues to Water Newton Lock some 3½ miles from Wansford Lock, where there is a telephone box just downstream of the lock on the road to the right, adjoining the mill and a postbox some 50 yards further on. The guillotine gate is now electrically powered.

At the lock, two mill streams discharge into the navigation channel immediately downstream of the structure and boaters are advised to keep to the right, when leaving the lock downstream, and use full power. The lock has a shallow lift and its approaches, both up and downstream, are ideal for mooring. A footbridge crosses here. The Hereward Way now turns north to cross the minor channels and join the road leading to Ailsworth. There is a picnic area and car park close to the downstream junction of the main and side channels on the left bank after the lock.

Water Newton church is a typical country church. It is approached by a private drive leading to the rectory. The church is dedicated to St Remigius, the Roman Bishop of Rheims. The 'water' in the name of the settlement is, of course, a reference to the Nene and to the east of the church is the old watermill, a three-storeyed mansard-roofed structure, now a dwelling, dating from 1791, adjacent to which is the former lock keeper's cottage. Nearby, at Sibson House, is the only survivor of a series of 'milestones' erected by Edmund Boulter. It is marked 'EB 1704' but is not a true milestone as no distances are indicated.

Once through Water Newton Lock, there is an upstream 'keep left' instruction adjoining Normangate Field Roman Potteries. The footpath now continues along the left bank of the Nene while the Nene/Hereward Way, having moved away from the river to the north for a short distance, then returns to run along the left bank of Back Dike, passing a further backwater on each bank. Just upstream of this point, the Nene is 'crossed' by the route of the Roman Road of Ermine Street which ran from London to York but no bridge to take the roadway now survives. As the Nene meanders southeast it passes the site of a Roman Town, Durobrivae, lying across the route of Ermine Street, to reach weirs at the westerly junctions of Back Dike and the Nene.

This immediate area contains much of historical interest. The village of Sutton is itself a conservation area and contains not only the site of the Sutton cross but also the Church of St Michael and All Angels, which was originally called St Giles. To the west of this church is a road which becomes a track leading to the Nene and formerly ran across an old ford to Stibbington. The crossing was however, unused for many years and was finally removed by the Nene River Board in the 1950s, to permit river traffic. The presence of Ermine Street is however the most interesting, confirming as it does the very significant Roman presence formerly in this area. The A1 follows much of the route of this road, which, as mentioned, crossed the Nene between Water Newton and Castor. Reference has already been made to Normangate Field Roman potteries and this hints at the presence, beside Ermine Street near Alwalton, of the remains of the Roman town of Durobrivae (the fort at the ford). This five-acre fort was centred around a courtyard which lay in the area of what is now the parish church, defended by a wall, bank and ditch. The boundaries of the town can still be picked out and aerial photographs show the irregular grid of streets set out slightly askew to Ermine Street.

The town was rediscovered when a small Roman camp, some ¼ mile to the north along Ermine Street, was being excavated by Edmund Artis, steward to the Earl Fitzwilliam, when a new estate road was being constructed in the nineteenth century. It was not however, until further excavations, by O G S Crawford in the 1930s, that the full significance of the find was realised. These excavations produced finds of pottery, coins and silver, including a find of first-century Christian silver, the earliest Christian religious silver found in the Roman Empire. In Roman times, there was a huge pottery industry centred between Billing Brook and where the A1 now runs, and local clay was used to produce Castorware, which was exported throughout the Empire.

Castor and Ailsworth

The modern settlements of Castor and Ailsworth on the left bank of the Nene are almost but not quite joined together, for, while there is no visible boundary between the villages, each has its own character, while sharing a church and school. 'Castor' is derived from the Roman word 'castra' meaning 'camp' and materials from Durobrivae were used to build the village church, which was founded in the seventh century and, uniquely in England, is dedicated to St Kyneburga, daughter of the founder, Penda King of Mercia. The church was largely rebuilt by the Normans, and over the chancel door is the latin inscription, 'this church was dedicated on April 17 1124'. On the north wall are three paintings, depicting the martyrdom of St Catherine. Pevsner described Castor Church as the most important Norman Parish Church in the county (of Huntingdon and Peterborough). Castor House, which stands to the east of the village, is Georgian. The Denver Causeway, which ran through the Fens left King Street, northwest of Castor at the south end of Moore Wood near Upton Church and joined, at Milton Park, another Roman road, leading back to the Nene Bridge at Castor. The route of this road can still be seen from the Peterborough Road, running through fields from the west side of Milton Park to Castor. It then passes through Peterborough, and eventually forms Low Road, Whittlesey, before moving into the fen. Large quantities of pottery were shipped from Castor in Roman times, via jetties on the Nene. For refreshments in Castor there are the following pubs and restaurants: The Prince of Wales Feathers (☎ 01733 380222), The Royal Oak (☎ 01733 390217) and Fratelli's Ristorante (the former Fitzwilliam Arms (☎ 01733 380251) all on the Peterborough Road through the village.

Ailsworth, on the other hand, is mainly of Saxon origin, although the site of a Roman villa, a house of the corridor type, has been found southwest of the station, beside the Nene, ½ mile upstream of the ford, following excavations in the nineteenth century. Its general layout is similar to Apethorpe (Northants).

The scenery is of peaceful willow-studded meadows, and Back Dike joins the Nene here by a series of channels and leads past Castor mill on the left bank, just downstream of which is the site of an old windmill. The Nene is forded and from here a footpath runs the short distance south between the channels to Alwalton Lock (two miles from Water Newton Lock) on the main channel. Here the Nene meets the outskirts of Peterborough, running close to the village/suburb of Alwalton and the East of England showground to the south. The Nene Way crosses Back Dike at the ford to run alongside the southern bank of the Dike. Here upstream of Alwalton Lock are the moorings of the Peterborough Cruising Club (☎ 01733 232739). A little way up the road from the lock, turning right at the top of this road, is Alwalton, where there is a post office/stores and the Cuckoo Inn (meals ☎ 01733 239638) and a telephone box on the road past the inn, leading to the A1. A footpath leads from Water End adjoining the inn, to the river.

Alwalton

Alwalton rather straggles up the A1. Sir Henry Royce, of the Rolls Royce car fame was born here and his ashes are now buried in the parish church, St Andrews.

In the 1860s Frank Perkins, who founded the engineering firm Perkins Engines lived in Alwalton. St Andrews has a thirteenth-century transept tower and a late twelfth-century south doorway. Northeast of the church is a cottage, bearing the date 1645 and northeast of this in turn is the porch of Chesterton, the manor of the poet John Dryden, demolished in 1867, but with the porch later rebuilt. The Manor House, northeast of the porch, dates from 1700. The mill which previously served Alwalton has gone but its leat remains and the high grown lynches on the southern bank of the river downstream of the mill leat mark the site of an ancient quarry, from which the Romans took marble.

The manor of Alwalton was given to the Abbey of Peterborough by Leofwine, ealdorman of Mercia, in the eleventh century and, in the Precentor's records at Peterborough, there are still ancient archives telling of the right to transport marble from Alwalton to Peterborough, free of boat and barge toll. This Alwalton marble was highly prized and a notable exhibit can be seen in the font bowl at Peterborough Cathedral.

From Alwalton to Peterborough, the Nene meanders partly through water meadows but the tree-lined banks in places hide the increasing urbanisation, particularly on the right bank, as the Alwalton Business Park and the suburbs of Orton are reached. The Nene passes the brickwork chimneys, with Peterborough Cathedral appearing above the tree tops. On the right bank immediately after Alwalton Lock, the Fitzwilliam estate has woods down to the water's edge but, once under the arch of the bridge carrying the private road to the Fitzwilliam kennels, the river is broad and the woods cease abruptly, with the skyline of the City of Peterborough in view.

At Alwalton Lock, where the guillotine gate is electrically powered, there is good access for canoes and after the lock both Back Dike and the Main Channel turn to the northeast, where the Main Channel is joined via a weir to a backwater. The Environment Agency are investigating the possibility of constructing moorings in this area.

The footpath from Castor Mill crosses the Nene at the Alwalton Road, while the Nene Way continues alongside the right bank of Back Dike until it rejoins the Main Nene, when it joins the left bank of the river as it turns to the north through a wooded section of bank between the Nene and the suburb of Orton Wistow, before being crossed on the left bank by the Nene Valley Railway. Between Alwalton and Orton Lock, is a four mile stretch through still pleasing countryside with the city views behind. The Nene turns east by Peterborough Golf Club, at Milton Park, on the left bank, to run close to the A47 trunk road, on that bank, before being crossed by Milton Ferry Bridge. This bridge marks the position of a former ferry. Boaters are advised to use the central arch of this bridge, where there is good headroom. Here, for a short while, urbanisation can be left behind. Milton Park is on the left bank with Nene Park on the right. Just to the west of Milton Park are two stones, referred to as Robin Hood and Little John. These mark the route by which Barnack Stone was taken to the river. Nene Park is a 2,500-acre regional park created along seven miles of the Nene from Peterborough City Centre to the A1. It is controlled by the Nene Park Trust and contains meadows, havens for wild flowers, and woods, fishing lakes, two golf courses, a watersports centre, a caravan club site and children's play area. Its centre piece is Ferry Meadows, three large (120 acres) connecting lakes formed by the extraction of sand and gravel between 1972–77. The lakes are Gunwade Lake, adjoining which are a café, information point and toilets, Lynch Lake, adjoining which are a car park and the Ferry Meadows station on the Nene Valley line, and Overton Lake, on which there are floating pontoon-type moorings and next to which is a caravan and camping area (☎ 01733 233526). Footpaths go right around the park, one running close to the right bank of the Nene, while the Nene Way, having crossed the Nene at the Milton Ferry Bridge, now runs along the northern side of Gunwade and Overton Lakes. The Hereward Way long-distance footpath runs along the left bank of the Nene, here. Milton Hall is on the left bank, in Milton Park.

On the Peterborough side of the Milton Ferry Bridge are woods and lynches and the Nene, having passed under this structure, now turns southeast to be crossed by the Bluebell footbridge. Here, the Nene Way crosses the channel, once again, to run along the left bank. The moorings and clubhouse of Peterborough Yacht Club are passed on the right bank and boaters are advised to travel slowly past the moored boats. Visitors are welcome. The slipway is for members only but there are Environment Agency short stay moorings. Thorpe Wood Club House and Golf Course lie on the left bank (☎ 01733 267701) and this and the neighbouring Orton Meadows Golf Course (☎ 01733 237478) are pay as you play. Adjacent is Thorpe Wood, a 20-acre site of ancient coppice and woodland.

Orton Lock some 4 miles downstream of Alwalton Lock, is an electrically-powered, vertical gate lock type. There are three substantial sluices immediately to the right of the lock chamber going downstream, which generate a very strong cross current. Boaters are advised to keep well to the right when leaving the lock and put on full power. These currents can also affect boats going upstream. There are bolts protruding downsteam of the lock and planned works to the structure will investigate these.In former times these sluices marked the upstream tidal limit of the Nene, until the building of the Dog-in-a-Doublet Sluice in 1938. The bank sides here are tree lined and give a somewhat false impression of rural tranquillity close to the city centre. The Nene Valley railway runs alongside the right bank of the Nene here to Orton Mere station, from where a footpath leads to the A605 and Orton Longueville 'village'. The 'village' has a post office/stores, shops and a postbox and telephone box at its entrance. It is also the site of Orton Hall, the ancestral home of the Gordon family, who held the titles of Marquess of Huntly and Earl of Aboyne. The doorway of Orton Hall is said to be from Fotheringhay Castle. In the grounds is also the Ramblewood Inn (☎ 01733 394444). While now effectively a 'Peterborough overspill' the village has a Roman connection and remains were discovered there in 1907. The church of Holy Trinity retains a bell from Plantagenet times and a sixteenth-century wall painting.

Downstream of Orton Lock boaters are advised to navigate with care due to the Proteus Canoe Club, which organises events on many weekends on this stretch which also contains a slalom course.

Flowing past the lakes on the right bank, the A1260 dual carriageway crosses the Nene downstream of the lock to cross the A605 on the right bank. The Nene turns northeast to pass Sculpture Park, on the left bank. This collection of sculptures is now owned and administered by the

Peterborough Sculpture Trust, after the demise of the original owners, Peterborough Development Corporation, in 1988. Adjacent to the park is the rowing course and the headquarters of Peterborough City Rowing Club, and the nearby Boathouse public house (☎ 01733 898469) where there are moorings for patrons and the Butterfly Hotel (☎ 01733 564240) can provide moorings and refreshments. This area is Thorpe Meadows and the Nene Valley Railway splits here, one line continuing to run alongside the right bank of the river. Nearby Thorpe Hall, built between 1653–6 by Peter Mills for Chief Justice St John is now a Sue Ryder Home, while St Augustine church, in the nearby parish of Woodston, has Anglo Saxon masonry in the west tower. Close by at Longthorpe, St Botolphs church has an interesting leper window and Longthorpe Tower, commissioned around 1300 by Robert de Thorpe, Steward of Peterborough Abbey, has walls between six and seven feet thick and, in the vaulted first floor great chamber, remarkable mid-fourteenth-century wall paintings on subjects taken from the bible and the contrast between worldly and spiritual life. The 'Wheel of the Five Senses' is particularly noteworthy. In the first century AD, a large Roman fort, some 28 acres in size stood near here on the left bank of the Nene. Its site is now part of the Thorpe Wood Golf Course.

The Nene passes more lakes, formed by former gravel workings, past Woodston and the adjoining suburb of New Fletton and, flanked by the railway on the right bank and the Nene Way on the left, it moves towards Peterborough City Centre.

As the crow flies, Northampton is only 36 miles from Peterborough but with the turns and twists of the Nene, a journey by river covers 58 miles.

Peterborough

Peterborough is the only Cathedral City on the Nene. Its earliest recorded name is Medeshamstede, (the meadow homestead) in AD655.

A Benedictine monastery was founded there in AD650 by Paeda, King of Mercia, which subsisted until the Reformation. It was an important Saxon religious centre, with the town growing up around it, but was destroyed by the Danes around AD820 and sacked again by Hereward the Wake 250 years later. The monastery stood where the cathedral now stands and excavations have revealed the remains of the Saxon church, which can be seen in the cathedral, below the present floor in the south transept. In the retro-choir of the cathedral is the Hedda Stone, a very important piece of Anglo-Saxon sculpture, dating from AD800. After its sacking by the Danes, the monastery was however rebuilt by St Aethelwold, who dedicated it to St Peter. By 972, the settlement was known as Burh (a defended settlement) but subsequently the town name took up the abbey's dedication. By 1225, the town was referred to as 'Burgus Sancti Petri' and, by 1333, Petreburgh. The present cathedral was built by the Normans, construction beginning in 1172. It is in the Anglo-Norman Romanesque style, with an early Gothic west front. Peterborough was raised to cathedral status in 1541 when Henry VIII dissolved the monasteries and housed the tombs of Catherine of Aragon, first wife of Henry VIII and Mary, Queen of Scots. The latter's son James I however, arranged for her body to be later removed to Westminster Abbey. It was effectively sacked by Cromwell's soldiers in 1643 and not fully restored until the 1890s, under the direction of J L Pearson. The cathedral has a painting of Robert Scarlett (otherwise known as Old Scarlett), verger there in the sixteenth century. He is pictured with a spade, pickaxe, keys and whip.

The Nene at Peterborough was first bridged by Godfrey of Croyland in 1308. The present bridge on this site, beside the Customs House, dates from 1934. Until 1801 Peterborough was a small town but the Industrial Revolution and the coming of the railway, together with the development of the brick industry following the discovery of Oxford Clay, stimulated growth. In 1968, the Peterborough Development Corporation was formed, the city received 'new town' designation and the population greatly increased. The latest development is the southern township, on old brickworkings. The great crested newt was discovered on the site, and were moved to part of the old brickworks, which has become an SSSI.

The City Centre is, with the exception of the cathedral, unfortunately architecturally poor. It does however contain all the facilities that can be expected of a large city with cafes, pubs, restaurants and a large variety of shops particularly in the Queensgate and Rivergate Centres. In the cathedral environs, however, there are a number of interesting buildings, historically important in their own right. The Precincts are entered from the Market Place, by the Outer Gate and to the south of this gate, vaults connect with the King's Lodgings and the Abbots Prison. The Abbots Gate dates from 1250 and there is a Norman arch from c1180, while a late-twelfth-century room survives in the garden to the east of Tort Hill mound, which was heaped up by Thorold, an eleventh-century abbot. There are also the impressive remains of the infirmary and two small nearby detached buildings. Table Hall, dating from the fifteenth century and the Infirmerers' Lodging from two centuries earlier. In addition the building known as the Vineyard marks the site of the mediaeval vineyard planted by Abbot Martin de Bec in c1140. Becket's Rest, in the cathedral grounds is a fourteenth century extension to a late Norman chapel dedicated to St Thomas, which has now been converted to a café and adjoins the Tourist Information facility (☎ 01733 452336). Away from the cathedral the Old Customs House, on Town Bridge, now the headquarters of the Sea Cadets and a scheduled ancient monument and the Old Guildhall, dating from 1671, on the market place, are also worth viewing.

Other features of interest in the Centre include Peterborough United FC on London Road, Peterborough Museum and Art Gallery, close to the cathedral in Priestgate and Railworld adjoining Town Bridge. This provides displays and exhibits (some 'hands on'), covering present and projected future train travel, the 'Age of Steam' and local railway displays and large locomotives (☎ 01733 344240).

Just upstream of Town Bridge, railway bridges cross the Nene and cables with a 10 feet minimum headroom also cross. There is also a new footbridge built in conjunction with a new riverside flats development. Here also is the Charters Barn and East Restaurant, advertised as being open every day. Just downstream of the bridge is Town Quay and Peterborough embankment, where there are moorings (port side only) and an amenity block, toilet, water and pump-out and rubbish disposal facilities. Keys to this facility are available from Peterborough Boating Centre at Stanground (☎ 01733 566688).

The embankment in Peterborough, downstream of Town Bridge and the main railway crossings, is a pleasant grassed area with walks, paved areas and shrubs. Town Bridge itself is a pleasant stone arched construction and just downstream is the Grain Barge floating restaurant where Chinese food can be obtained (☎ 01733 311967). The Nene is wide here and overhung with trees on the right bank, which is piled for a short distance. The Embankment contains the Millennium Field of Hope, sponsored by a number of local organisations and there is significant space for the short term 48-hour moorings under the jurisdiction of Peterborough City Council just downstream of the Key Theatre.

The sunken barge *Lauria* has now been removed from its location opposite the embankment. During this operation the opportunity was taken to remove a number of shopping trollies and other refuse. Asda, whose premises front the river, have announced the introduction of new technology, which should help to alleviate this problem. Here also are Charter Cruise River Trips and, nearby, a sign reminding boaters of the need to register with the Environment Agency.

The Key Ferry offers river trips from the left bank (☎ 01733 393972) while the Key Theatre (box office ☎ 01733 552439 open 1000–2000 Mon–Sat) provides an established entertainment venue and includes the Riverside Bar and Key Coffee Shop. Next to the theatre is the Peterborough City Council slipway. From here the floodlights of the ground of Peterborough United FC on London Road are visible to the right. There is a short industrial vista on the right bank, where some 'de facto' mooring takes place, in contrast to the gardens of the embankment on the left, behind which the cathedral is visible. Fishing is generally allowed from the embankment except where yellow indications sign a prohibition. There is good canoe access and parking facilities.

Peterborough to the Sea

Life never presents us with anything which may not be looked upon as a fresh starting point, no less than as a termination'
André Gide

After Peterborough Embankment is left behind, the river takes on a more natural look as the A1139 road bridge is approached although the presence of electricity pylons is very noticeable and the bridge itself can only be described as functional. In truth however, the original Nene channel is extinct in this reach as it has been replaced by the straight lengths of the 'Fen Drayners'.

After this bridge, the spire of Stanground Church can be seen on the right.

To the left is a signpost designating the Green Wheel and Flag Fen. The Green Wheel is modern and the work of the Peterborough Environment City Trust. It provides not only a circular cycle track around the city but also 'spokes' of the 'wheel', coming out from various points in the city to join the main 'circle'. It is an attempt by the Trust to encourage both leisure and commuting use of cycles and is to be commended.

Flag Fen is at almost the other end of the historical time scale. The site is on a gravel promentory beside the Nene and was occupied from Neolithic to Roman times. It is bounded on the west by a section of the old Roman Car Dyke and inhumations from the Beaker Period and cremations in urns from the Middle Bronze Age have been found, as well as Iron Age material. The damp nature of the soil has acted as a preservative of much of the remains and the reconstructed Iron Age village on the site is a major tourist attraction. It was discovered in 1982, when the archaeologist Frances Pryor came across a protruding oak stump disturbed by an excavator. The site was known to be crossed by the Roman Fen Causeway but this stump had been worked to form a post and placed three feet below the level of the Roman road. Excavation of the site revealed thousands of timbers, perfectly preserved by immersion in the acidic waterlogged peat. They composed part of a platform estimated to be about the size of two football pitches with the remains of buildings upon it, which had been built out in the shallow waters of the Fen in the late Bronze Age. Before the great drainage works of the seventeenth century, this had been a wild and watery landscape, but one which the twelfth-century writer Hugh Candidus recorded offered an 'abundance (of) all things needful for them that dwell nearby'. People had settled on the Fen edge since at least Neolithic times (c4000–2000 BC).

Pryor's next major discovery, in 1989, concerned a structure of posts running for over ½ mile in length across and beyond the platform. At first he thought it could be a causeway linking the platform with dry land, but it became apparent that it had been constructed after the platform had been abandoned because of rising water levels, perhaps as some kind of barrier. On the seaward side was unearthed a remarkable collection of metal artefacts, which included swords, daggers, tools and helmets which appeared to have been ceremonially buried as grave goods.

Modern drainage of the Fens has reduced the ground level in places by as much as 13' in the last 100 years. Drying out is a severe threat to Flag Fen, so a lake has been formed over part of the site, to preserve the unexcavated part of the platform which lies beneath it.

Flag Fen is an active archaeological park and the reconstructed village includes authentic style outhouses, round houses and a mere. Its museum contains the oldest wheel found in England, and 3,000 year old timbers, still with the original marks of the tools that furbished them so long ago. Excavations have also revealed an intact Roman road. Flag Fen has a Visitor Centre, exhibition, café and gift shop and is open from 1000–1700 (☎ 01733 313414).

The Nene divides with Mortons Leam moving off to the southeast and crossing under the Nene Valley Railway line running east, while the main channel continues to the northeast.

Mortons Leam and the Middle Level

Mortons Leam, constructed under the auspices of Bishop Morton of Ely, in the fourteenth century, was one of the earliest attempts to better drain this area of the fens by the provision of a longer straighter cut, for the quicker conveyance of flood waters.

It rejoins the main channel of the Nene at Guyhirn and, between it and the main Nene, are the Nene Washes. This 600-acre area was constructed in the seventeenth century as a flood storage area to hold excess water from the river in times of high flow, as part of the 'Great Drayning' Scheme designed for the Earl of Bedford by Cornelius Vermuyden. The Washes still retain that function today but, in addition, have become an important wildfowl and wildlife site, especially for birds (in particular black tailed godwit, duck, lapwing and redshank) and much of the site is an RSPB reserve. Traditional management practices to retain both the flood storage use and conservation designation are encouraged.

In entering Mortons Leam care should be taken in navigating Black Bridge, the railway bridge carrying the Nene Valley railway, as three of the bridge pillars are in the waterway. Both arches are, however, navigable.

Mortons Leam provides the route to Stanground and entry via the manned Stanground Lock (☎ 01733 566413) lock-keeper's cottage on the right bank) to the Middle Level River system. The upstream landing stage just prior to Stanground Lock has been recently refurbished Those wishing to enter the Middle Level system should give the lock-keeper 48 hours notice of their intention to do so. (The Middle Level Commissioners' main number is 01354 653232). Stanground village has shops and a pub, the Woolpack (☎ 01733 554417 meals). Historically, prior to the 'Great Drayning' of the seventeenth century, the route through Stanground was the course of the Nene.

On Mortons Leam, just before Stanground Lock, are two boatyards, Jacksons (☎ 01733 560645) and Peterborough Boating Centre where use of the private slipway might be permitted (☎ 01733 566688) both on the right bank.

The main Nene continues northeast from its junction with Mortons Leam, with the Nene Way still on its left bank. The Nene is now uniformly wide and deep. Peterborough Greyhound Stadium stands on the left bank, and the Nene passes this just before Fitzwilliam Bridge crosses the river, a slightly more pleasing structure than the High Road Bridge, which carries the A1139.

Here the embankment opens out on the left bank into a wider grassy tree lined area. The right bank has a softer more natural look and opens out on to meadows. To the rear, views of Peterborough Cathedral can still be seen. The river from here to the sea is now embanked to protect its waters from spilling over into the adjoining low fen ground, most of which lies at or below sea level, in total contrast to the valley, through which the river previously passed.

Downstream of the Fitzwilliam Bridge, the normal speed limit of 11·2kph/7mph is removed for the next mile to allow water skiing to take place on a straight section of the river. The water skiing course is clearly signed at both ends but caution is obviously required when navigating this length. At the end of this mile, are two bends in the river before a straight two mile stretch marks the end of the unrestricted area and the river turns slightly north to pass the Flag Fen sewage works and the Flag Fen excavations and museum. The minor road from Eye runs along the left bank for a short distance with former sand pit lakes on the landward side of it.

The footpath continues on the left bank but the countryside has now changed dramatically to reflect the fenland river that the Nene has now become. The 'real Nene' can therefore be said to end at Peterborough. From now on, to the sea, the river conveys upland water through artificial cuts to its outfall. These cuts run between the steep embankments, with the flat fen lands and isolated farm buildings as scenery.

Compared to the proliferation of wooded areas upstream, the lack of trees now is very noticeable. The embanked stretch also marks the end of the fluvial Nene as it approaches Dog-in-a-Doublet Lock, where the B1040 road from Whittlesey to Thorney crosses and, just off this road, is Northey Lodge Campsite and Caravan park (☎ 01733 223918) where storage of boats either for long periods (6 months–1year) or during the week is available. There are no moorings, but a DIY facility for boat washing or minor repairs.

The lock at Dog-in-a-Doublet was built in 1938 and is manned during daylight hours (☎ 01733 202219). In addition to being a lock, it acts as a sluice to protect Peterborough from tidal inundation. Save for vessels seeking passage through the lock, there is no mooring allowed within 100m of the structure but a 48-hour mooring has been installed upstream of the lock. The structure also has a high tech fish pass, installed in 1998. The nearby Dog-in-a-Doublet public house (☎ 01733 202256) has a restaurant and provides bar meals and there are general facilities to be found in Whittlesey, one mile to the south.

The derivation of the name 'Dog-in-a-Doublet' is interesting. The pub was one of several erected along the Nene in the mid 1700s by the Bedford Level Corporation, then responsible for the river and one of the early publicans also served as lock-keeper and as a decoy man, working the local duck decoys. It is said that a terrier dog that he used to help him with this last mentioned work contracted a skin disease, through which it lost its fur and that following this, the publican's wife made it a leather jerkin to keep it warm, hence 'Dog-in-a-Doublet'.

Whittlesey

Whittlesey is best known for its brickworks and the towering chimneys of the kilns are landmarks for miles around. In prehistoric times the sea covered these parts and a number of significant marine fossils have been unearthed, including, in September 1987, that of a 160 million year old plesiosaur. This is now in Peterborough Museum. Four miles below Whittlesey is Poplar House Farm, where the Nene bisects the Greenwich Meridian. There is also a buried Roman causeway here, that once linked Goosetree with Eldernell.

Below the Dog-in-a-Doublet Lock the river is tidal and comparatively uninteresting with mooring being much more difficult, although the Nene still has a further 25 miles to travel to reach the sea. Craft may pass through the lock every day from 7.30 am until sunset, although boat owners are advised to phone the lock-keeper in advance to arrange for passage. On the tidal stretch, there are only the settlements of Guyhirn, where a tidal mooring has been installed, eight miles downstream and just above where Mortons Leam rejoins the right bank of the Nene at the end of the Nene Washes, Wisbech, some seven miles further on and Sutton Bridge, eight miles still further downstream, almost as the Nene enters the Wash. For anyone voyaging to the extremity of the Nene, at West lighthouses, there is a two hour tide differential from Dog-in-a-Doublet.

The headroom clearance at Guyhirn Road Bridge, varies with the tide, while craft should proceed through Wisbech with care as the bank is lined with steel and concrete piling, there is stoning in the bed and a strong run on flood and ebb tides, particularly in the lower stages. For information on the passage of craft through and moorings in Wisbech and down to the sea, the Port Manager at Wisbech should be consulted (☎ 01945 588059). Although the river is less interesting here, Wisbech has a fine display of Georgian architecture on the North Brink of the Nene, recognising the importance of the port over many centuries, although the storehouses and boat building yards that previously stood close to Town Bridge have long gone. Indeed, before land reclamation and coastal changes, Wisbech was once on the coast. It was also the home of Thomas Clarkson, who played a major part in the fight for the abolition of slavery and of Octavia Hill, co-founder of the National Trust. Below Wisbech, the flow of the Nene through the reclaimed land divides Norfolk from Lincolnshire and, between Wisbech and Sutton Bridge, the main drains of the North Level and South Holland Internal Drainage Boards discharge on the left bank just before the port of Sutton Bridge is reached (Port Office ☎ 01406 351133). Beyond Sutton Bridge lies the sea and for the Nene, the end of its journey.

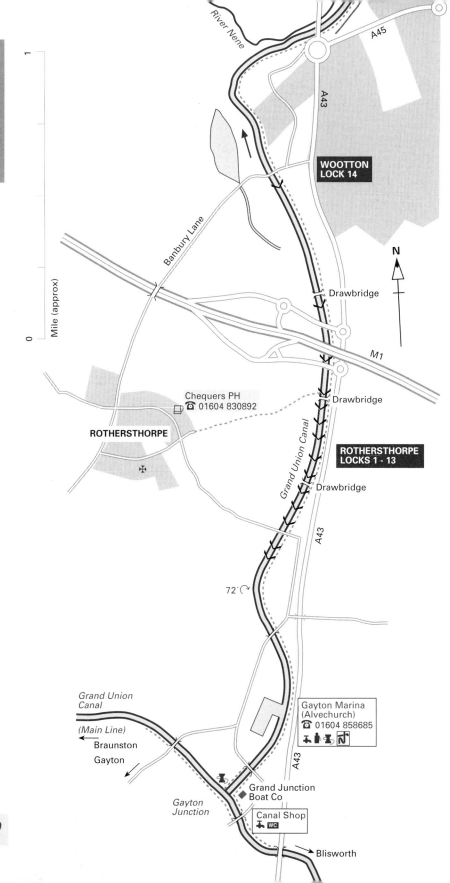

River Nene

A45

A43

1

Mile (approx)

0

WOOTTON LOCK 14

Banbury Lane

Drawbridge

N

M1

Chequers PH
☐ ☎ 01604 830892

ROTHERSTHORPE

Drawbridge

Grand Union Canal

ROTHERSTHORPE LOCKS 1 - 13

Drawbridge

A43

72′ ↻

Grand Union
Canal

(Main Line)
← Braunston
Gayton

Gayton Marina
(Alvechurch)
☎ 01604 858685

A43

Gayton
Junction

Grand Junction
Boat Co

Canal Shop
WC

→ Blisworth

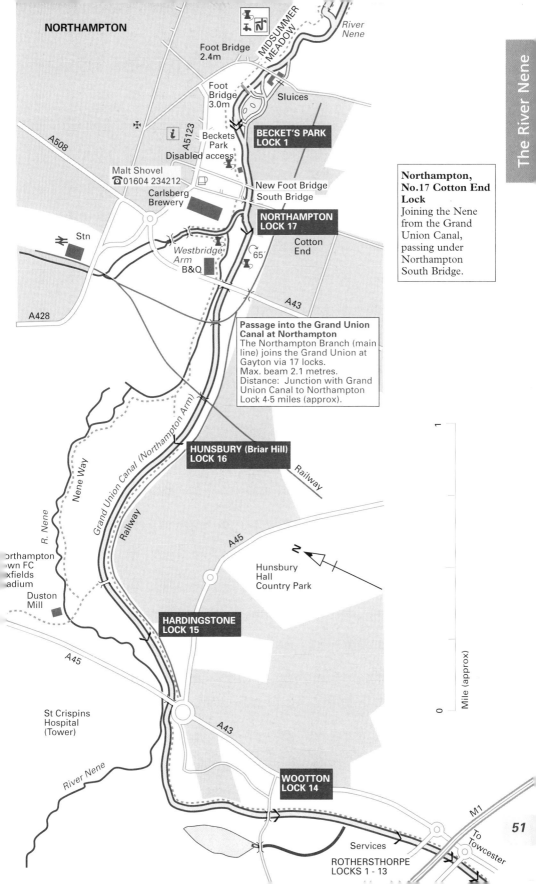

NORTHAMPTON

River Nene

MIDSUMMER MEADOW

Foot Bridge 2.4m

Foot Bridge 3.0m

Sluices

Beckets Park

BECKET'S PARK LOCK 1

Disabled access

A5123

A508

Malt Shovel
☎ 01604 234212

Carlsberg Brewery

New Foot Bridge
South Bridge

NORTHAMPTON LOCK 17

Stn

Westbridge Arm

B&Q

65

Cotton End

A43

A428

Northampton, No.17 Cotton End Lock
Joining the Nene from the Grand Union Canal, passing under Northampton South Bridge.

Passage into the Grand Union Canal at Northampton
The Northampton Branch (main line) joins the Grand Union at Gayton via 17 locks.
Max. beam 2.1 metres.
Distance: Junction with Grand Union Canal to Northampton Lock 4·5 miles (approx).

Grand Union Canal (Northampton Arm)

HUNSBURY (Briar Hill) LOCK 16

Railway

Nene Way

Railway

R. Nene

orthampton
wn FC
xfields
adium

Duston Mill

A45

Hunsbury Hall Country Park

N

HARDINGSTONE LOCK 15

A45

1

Mile (approx)

0

St Crispins Hospital (Tower)

A43

River Nene

WOOTTON LOCK 14

M1

To Towcester

51

Services

ROTHERSTHORPE LOCKS 1 - 13

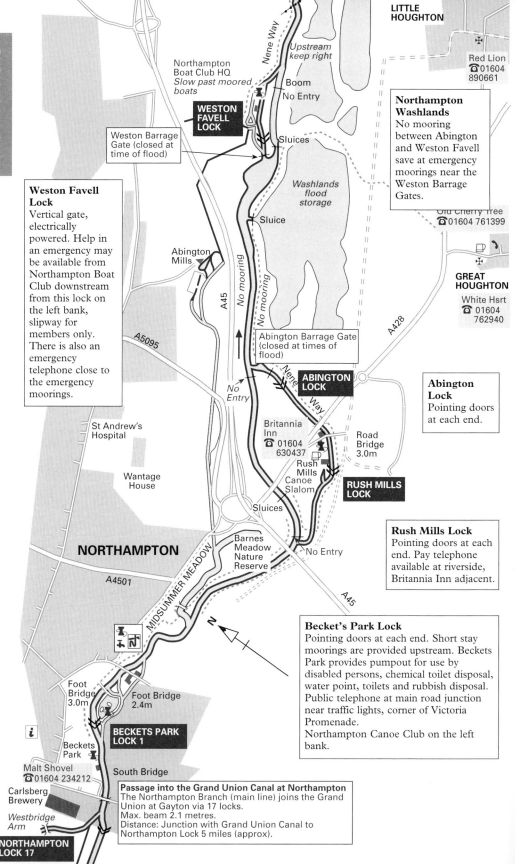

LITTLE HOUGHTON

Nene Way

Upstream keep right

Northampton Boat Club HQ
Slow past moored boats

Boom
No Entry

WESTON FAVELL LOCK

Weston Barrage Gate (closed at time of flood)

Sluices

Red Lion
☎ 01604 890661

Northampton Washlands
No mooring between Abington and Weston Favell save at emergency moorings near the Weston Barrage Gates.

Washlands flood storage

Sluice

Weston Favell Lock
Vertical gate, electrically powered. Help in an emergency may be available from Northampton Boat Club downstream from this lock on the left bank, slipway for members only. There is also an emergency telephone close to the emergency moorings.

Old Cherry Tree
☎ 01604 761399

GREAT HOUGHTON

White Hsrt
☎ 01604 762940

Abington Mills

A45

A5095

No mooring

No mooring

Abington Barrage Gate (closed at times of flood)

Nene Way

No Entry

ABINGTON LOCK

A428

Abington Lock
Pointing doors at each end.

St Andrew's Hospital

Wantage House

Britannia Inn
☎ 01604 630437

Rush Mills Canoe Slalom

Road Bridge 3.0m

RUSH MILLS LOCK

Rush Mills Lock
Pointing doors at each end. Pay telephone available at riverside, Britannia Inn adjacent.

NORTHAMPTON

A4501

MIDSUMMER MEADOW

Barnes Meadow Nature Reserve

Sluices

No Entry

A45

N

Becket's Park Lock
Pointing doors at each end. Short stay moorings are provided upstream. Beckets Park provides pumpout for use by disabled persons, chemical toilet disposal, water point, toilets and rubbish disposal. Public telephone at main road junction near traffic lights, corner of Victoria Promenade.
Northampton Canoe Club on the left bank.

Foot Bridge 3.0m

Foot Bridge 2.4m

BECKETS PARK LOCK 1

i

Beckets Park

Malt Shovel
☎ 01604 234212

South Bridge

Carlsberg Brewery

Westbridge Arm

NORTHAMPTON LOCK 17

Passage into the Grand Union Canal at Northampton
The Northampton Branch (main line) joins the Grand Union at Gayton via 17 locks.
Max. beam 2.1 metres.
Distance: Junction with Grand Union Canal to Northampton Lock 5 miles (approx).

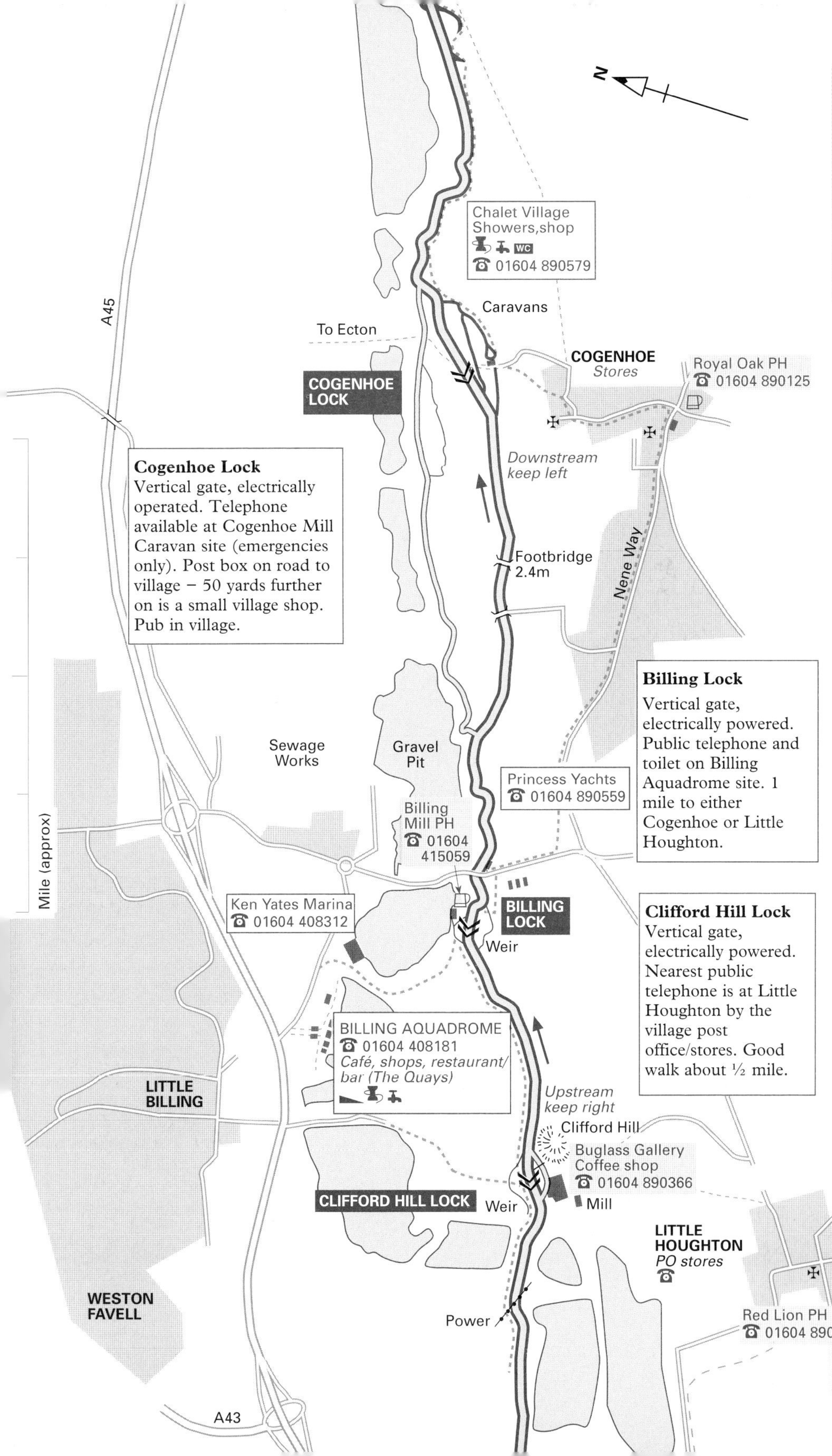

N

Chalet Village
Showers, shop
☎ 01604 890579

Caravans

To Ecton

COGENHOE
Stores

Royal Oak PH
☎ 01604 890125

COGENHOE
LOCK

Cogenhoe Lock
Vertical gate, electrically
operated. Telephone
available at Cogenhoe Mill
Caravan site (emergencies
only). Post box on road to
village – 50 yards further
on is a small village shop.
Pub in village.

*Downstream
keep left*

Footbridge
2.4m

Nene Way

Billing Lock
Vertical gate,
electrically powered.
Public telephone and
toilet on Billing
Aquadrome site. 1
mile to either
Cogenhoe or Little
Houghton.

Sewage
Works

Gravel
Pit

Princess Yachts
☎ 01604 890559

Billing
Mill PH
☎ 01604
415059

Ken Yates Marina
☎ 01604 408312

**BILLING
LOCK**

Clifford Hill Lock
Vertical gate,
electrically powered.
Nearest public
telephone is at Little
Houghton by the
village post
office/stores. Good
walk about ½ mile.

Weir

BILLING AQUADROME
☎ 01604 408181
*Café, shops, restaurant/
bar (The Quays)*

**LITTLE
BILLING**

*Upstream
keep right*

Clifford Hill

Buglass Gallery
Coffee shop
☎ 01604 890366

CLIFFORD HILL LOCK Weir

Mill

**LITTLE
HOUGHTON**
PO stores
☎

**WESTON
FAVELL**

Power

Red Lion PH
☎ 01604 890661

Mile (approx)

A45

A43

53

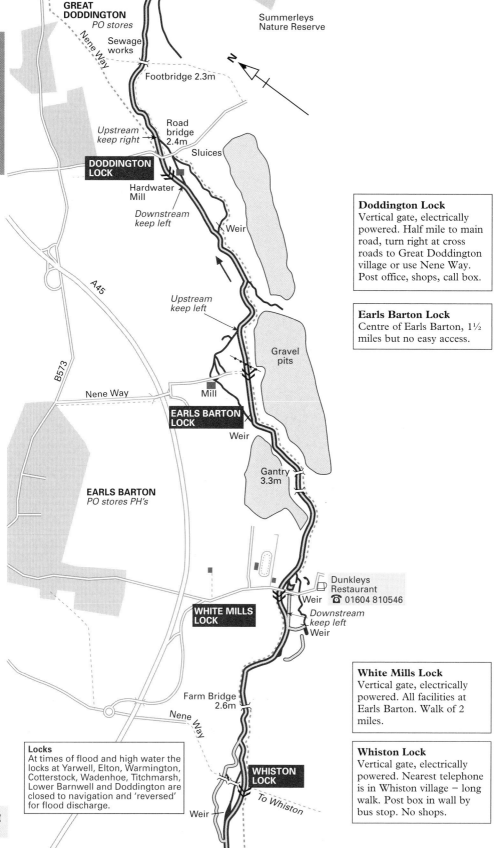

GREAT DODDINGTON
PO stores

Summerleys
Nature Reserve

Sewage
works

Nene Way

N

Footbridge 2.3m

*Upstream
keep right*

Road
bridge
2.4m

Sluices

**DODDINGTON
LOCK**

Hardwater
Mill

*Downstream
keep left*

Weir

A45

*Upstream
keep left*

Gravel
pits

B573

Nene Way

Mill

**EARLS BARTON
LOCK**

Weir

Gantry
3.3m

EARLS BARTON
PO stores PH's

Dunkleys
Restaurant
☎ 01604 810546

Weir

**WHITE MILLS
LOCK**

*Downstream
keep left*

Weir

Farm Bridge
2.6m

Nene Way

**WHISTON
LOCK**

To Whiston

Weir

Doddington Lock
Vertical gate, electrically powered. Half mile to main road, turn right at cross roads to Great Doddington village or use Nene Way. Post office, shops, call box.

Earls Barton Lock
Centre of Earls Barton, 1½ miles but no easy access.

White Mills Lock
Vertical gate, electrically powered. All facilities at Earls Barton. Walk of 2 miles.

Whiston Lock
Vertical gate, electrically powered. Nearest telephone is in Whiston village − long walk. Post box in wall by bus stop. No shops.

Locks
At times of flood and high water the locks at Yarwell, Elton, Warmington, Cotterstock, Wadenhoe, Titchmarsh, Lower Barnwell and Doddington are closed to navigation and 'reversed' for flood discharge.

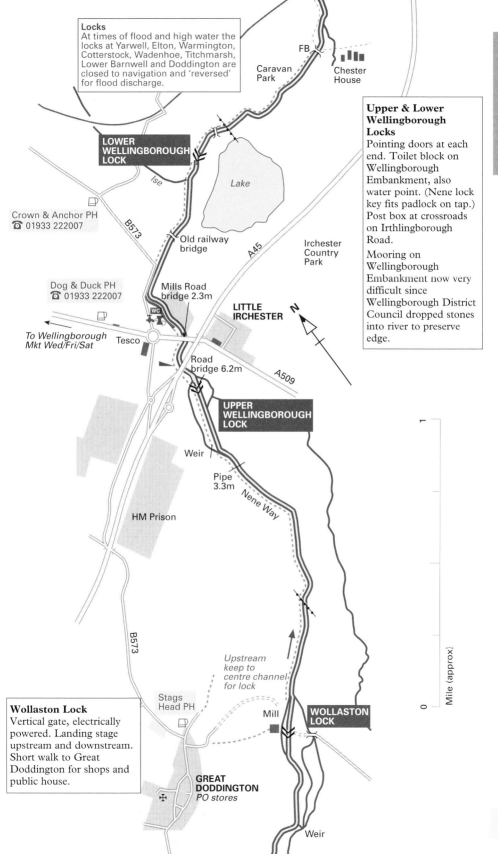

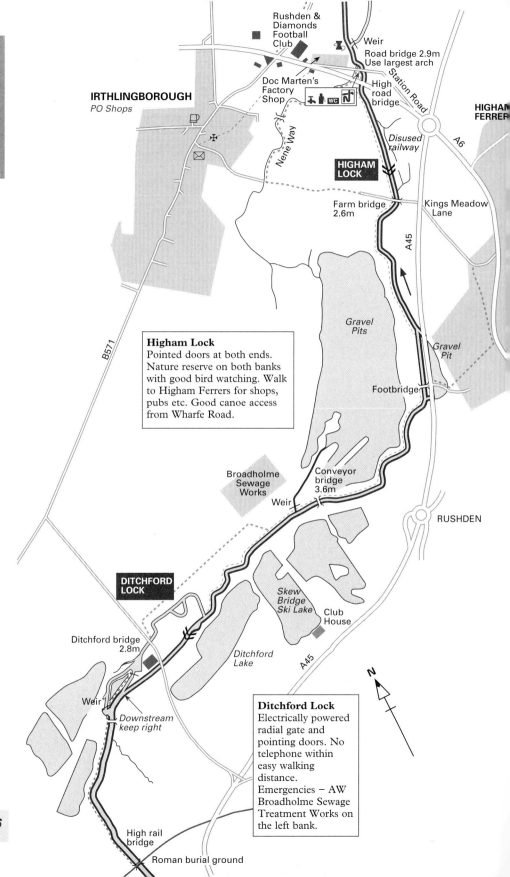

Rushden &
Diamonds
Football
Club

Weir
Road bridge 2.9m
Use largest arch

IRTHLINGBOROUGH
PO Shops

Doc Marten's
Factory
Shop

High
road
bridge

Station Road

HIGHAM
FERRER

A6

Nene Way

*Disused
railway*

**HIGHAM
LOCK**

Farm bridge
2.6m

Kings Meadow
Lane

A45

*Gravel
Pits*

*Gravel
Pit*

Higham Lock
Pointed doors at both ends.
Nature reserve on both banks
with good bird watching. Walk
to Higham Ferrers for shops,
pubs etc. Good canoe access
from Wharfe Road.

Footbridge

Broadholme
Sewage
Works

Conveyor
bridge
3.6m

Weir

RUSHDEN

**DITCHFORD
LOCK**

*Skew
Bridge
Ski Lake*

Club
House

Ditchford bridge
2.8m

*Ditchford
Lake*

A45

N

Weir

*Downstream
keep right*

Ditchford Lock
Electrically powered
radial gate and
pointing doors. No
telephone within
easy walking
distance.
Emergencies – AW
Broadholme Sewage
Treatment Works on
the left bank.

B571

High rail
bridge

Roman burial ground

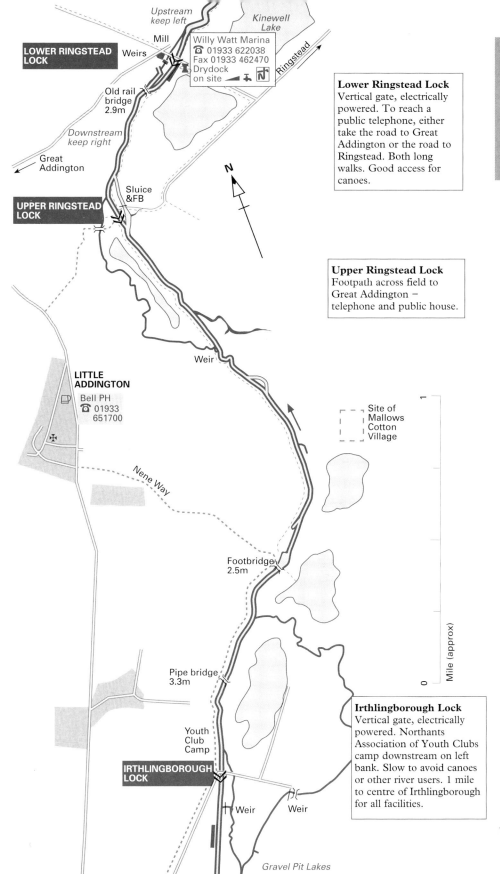

LOWER RINGSTEAD LOCK

Upstream keep left

Kinewell Lake

Mill

Weirs

Willy Watt Marina
☎ 01933 622038
Fax 01933 462470
Drydock on site

Ringstead

Old rail bridge 2.9m

Downstream keep right

Great Addington

N

Lower Ringstead Lock
Vertical gate, electrically powered. To reach a public telephone, either take the road to Great Addington or the road to Ringstead. Both long walks. Good access for canoes.

Sluice &FB

UPPER RINGSTEAD LOCK

Upper Ringstead Lock
Footpath across field to Great Addington – telephone and public house.

Weir

LITTLE ADDINGTON
Bell PH
☎ 01933 651700

Site of Mallows Cotton Village

Nene Way

Footbridge 2.5m

Mile (approx)

1

0

Pipe bridge 3.3m

Youth Club Camp

IRTHLINGBOROUGH LOCK

Weir   Weir

Irthlingborough Lock
Vertical gate, electrically powered. Northants Association of Youth Clubs camp downstream on left bank. Slow to avoid canoes or other river users. 1 mile to centre of Irthlingborough for all facilities.

Gravel Pit Lakes

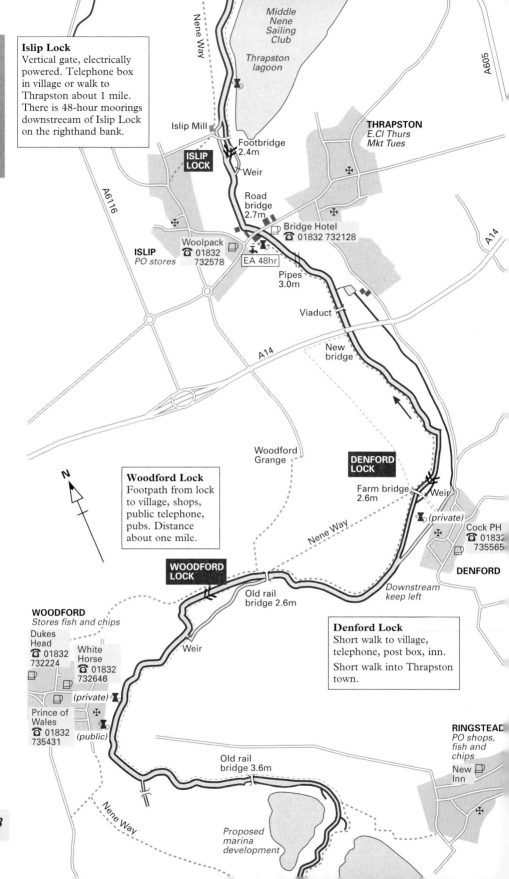

Islip Lock
Vertical gate, electrically powered. Telephone box in village or walk to Thrapston about 1 mile. There is 48-hour moorings downstreeam of Islip Lock on the righthand bank.

Nene Way

Middle Nene Sailing Club

Thrapston lagoon

A605

Islip Mill

THRAPSTON
E.Cl Thurs Mkt Tues

Footbridge 2.4m

ISLIP LOCK

Weir

Road bridge 2.7m

Bridge Hotel ☎ 01832 732128

A14

ISLIP
PO stores

Woolpack ☎ 01832 732578

EA 48hr

Pipes 3.0m

Viaduct

A6116

A14

New bridge

Woodford Grange

DENFORD LOCK

Farm bridge 2.6m

Weir

(private)

Cock PH ☎ 01832 735565

DENFORD

N

Woodford Lock
Footpath from lock to village, shops, public telephone, pubs. Distance about one mile.

Nene Way

WOODFORD LOCK

Old rail bridge 2.6m

Downstream keep left

WOODFORD
Stores fish and chips

Dukes Head ☎ 01832 732224

White Horse ☎ 01832 732646

(private)

Prince of Wales ☎ 01832 735431

(public)

Weir

Denford Lock
Short walk to village, telephone, post box, inn.

Short walk into Thrapston town.

RINGSTEAD
PO shops, fish and chips

New Inn

Old rail bridge 3.6m

Nene Way

Proposed marina development

58

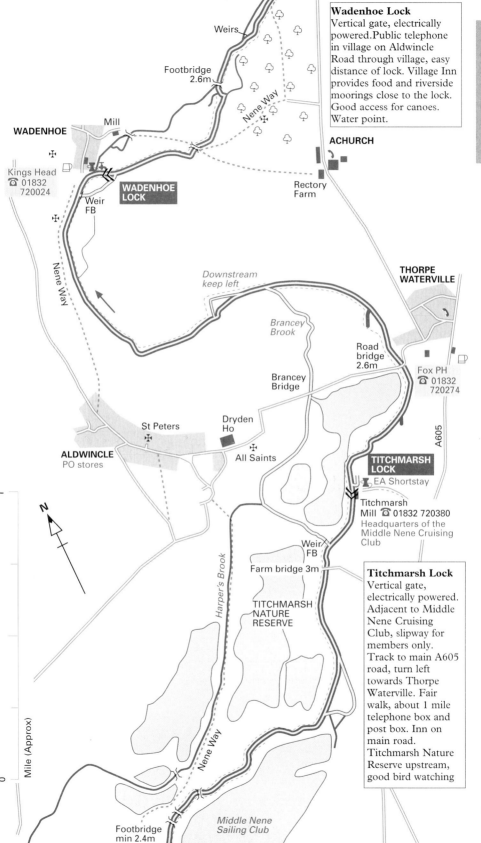

Wadenhoe Lock
Vertical gate, electrically powered. Public telephone in village on Aldwincle Road through village, easy distance of lock. Village Inn provides food and riverside moorings close to the lock. Good access for canoes. Water point.

Weirs

Footbridge
2.6m

Nene Way

Mill

ACHURCH

WADENHOE

Kings Head
☎ 01832
720024

WADENHOE
LOCK

Weir
FB

Rectory
Farm

Nene Way

Downstream
keep left

THORPE
WATERVILLE

Brancey
Brook

Road
bridge
2.6m

Fox PH
☎ 01832
720274

Brancey
Bridge

A605

Dryden
Ho

St Peters

ALDWINCLE
PO stores

All Saints

TITCHMARSH
LOCK

EA Shortstay

Titchmarsh
Mill ☎ 01832 720380
Headquarters of the
Middle Nene Cruising
Club

N

1

Mile (Approx)

0

Harper's Brook

Weir
FB

Farm bridge 3m

TITCHMARSH
NATURE
RESERVE

Nene Way

Titchmarsh Lock
Vertical gate, electrically powered. Adjacent to Middle Nene Cruising Club, slipway for members only. Track to main A605 road, turn left towards Thorpe Waterville. Fair walk, about 1 mile telephone box and post box. Inn on main road. Titchmarsh Nature Reserve upstream, good bird watching

Footbridge
min 2.4m

Middle Nene
Sailing Club

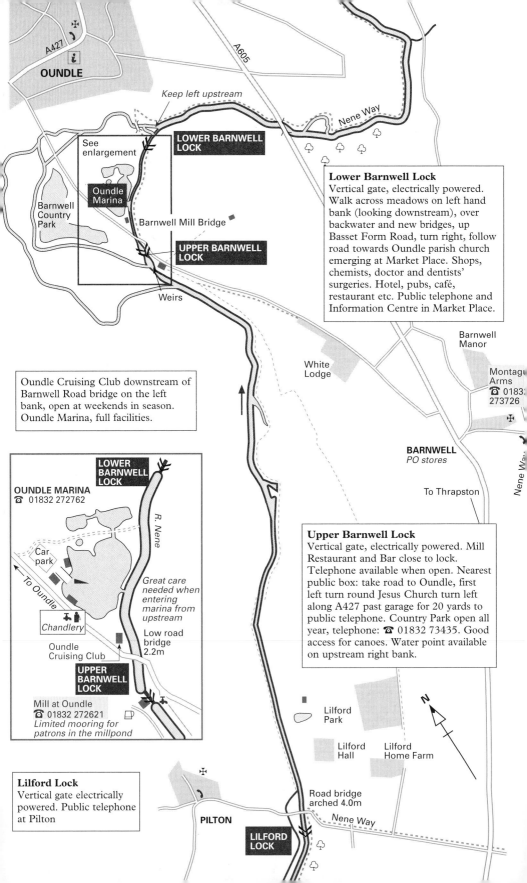

OUNDLE

A427

A605

Keep left upstream

LOWER BARNWELL LOCK

See enlargement

Oundle Marina

Barnwell Country Park

Barnwell Mill Bridge

UPPER BARNWELL LOCK

Weirs

Nene Way

Lower Barnwell Lock
Vertical gate, electrically powered. Walk across meadows on left hand bank (looking downstream), over backwater and new bridges, up Basset Form Road, turn right, follow road towards Oundle parish church emerging at Market Place. Shops, chemists, doctor and dentists' surgeries. Hotel, pubs, café, restaurant etc. Public telephone and Information Centre in Market Place.

Barnwell Manor

Montagu Arms
☎ 0183 273726

White Lodge

BARNWELL
PO stores

To Thrapston

Oundle Cruising Club downstream of Barnwell Road bridge on the left bank, open at weekends in season. Oundle Marina, full facilities.

LOWER BARNWELL LOCK

OUNDLE MARINA
☎ 01832 272762

Car park

To Oundle

R. Nene

Great care needed when entering marina from upstream

Chandlery

Oundle Cruising Club

Low road bridge 2.2m

UPPER BARNWELL LOCK

Mill at Oundle
☎ 01832 272621
Limited mooring for patrons in the millpond

Upper Barnwell Lock
Vertical gate, electrically powered. Mill Restaurant and Bar close to lock. Telephone available when open. Nearest public box: take road to Oundle, first left turn round Jesus Church turn left along A427 past garage for 20 yards to public telephone. Country Park open all year, telephone: ☎ 01832 73435. Good access for canoes. Water point available on upstream right bank.

N

Lilford Park

Lilford Hall

Lilford Home Farm

Lilford Lock
Vertical gate electrically powered. Public telephone at Pilton

PILTON

Road bridge arched 4.0m

Nene Way

LILFORD LOCK

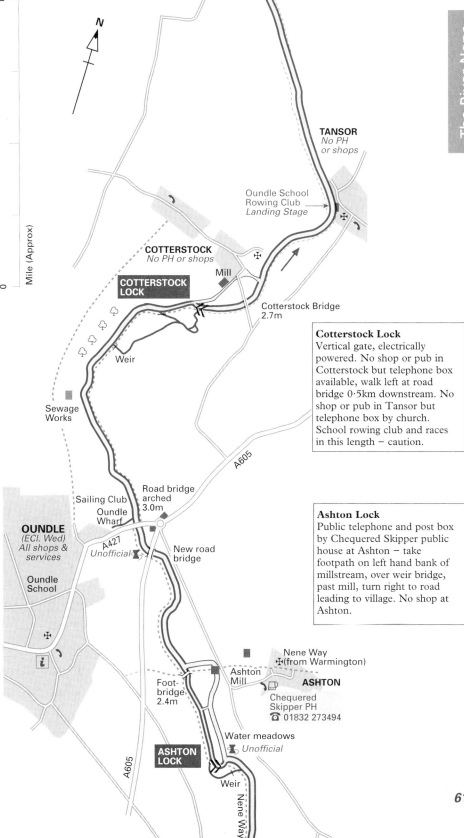

Mile (Approx)

N

TANSOR
*No PH
or shops*

Oundle School
Rowing Club
→ *Landing Stage*

COTTERSTOCK
No PH or shops

Mill

**COTTERSTOCK
LOCK**

Cotterstock Bridge
2.7m

Weir

Sewage
Works

A605

Cotterstock Lock
Vertical gate, electrically
powered. No shop or pub in
Cotterstock but telephone box
available, walk left at road
bridge 0·5km downstream. No
shop or pub in Tansor but
telephone box by church.
School rowing club and races
in this length – caution.

Road bridge
arched
3.0m

Sailing Club
Oundle
Wharf

OUNDLE
*(ECl. Wed)
All shops &
services*

A427
Unofficial

New road
bridge

Oundle
School

i

Ashton Lock
Public telephone and post box
by Chequered Skipper public
house at Ashton – take
footpath on left hand bank of
millstream, over weir bridge,
past mill, turn right to road
leading to village. No shop at
Ashton.

Nene Way
(from Warmington)

Ashton
Mill

ASHTON

Foot-
bridge
2.4m

Chequered
Skipper PH
☎ 01832 273494

A605

Water meadows
Unofficial

**ASHTON
LOCK**

Weir

Nene Way

Nene Way

61

Sewage works

Elton
Road bridge
3.3m

Crown Inn
☎ 01832 280232

ELTON
LOCK

Black Horse Inn
☎ 01832 280240

Mill

ELTON
PO stores

Elton Lock
Vertical gate electrically powered. Path from lock leads to village green. Middle Street leading to main A605 road. Village store/Post office with telephone box in Middle Street. Crown Inn on Duck Street.

Weir

Elton
Park

Willow Brook

Mile (Approx)

1

0

Warmington Lock
Footpath across meadows towards Elton Boat Club (boats moored on Mill Stream), walk past mill to Eaglethorpe, across main road (A605) into Warmington via Chapel Street, first turn on right leads to store, post office, telephone box. Pillar box opposite Red Lion also on A605. Good access for canoes via the Mill. Short stay moorings and water point available at the boat club.

N

Upstream
keep right

A605

WARMINGTO
PO Stores

WARMINGTON
LOCK

Red Lion PH
☎ 01832 280362

FOTHERINGHAY

Castle
Mound

Nene Way

Eagle
thorpe
Mill

Falcon PH
☎ 01832
226254

Weir
FB

Elton Boat
Club HQ

Nene Way

To
Nassington

Fotheringhay Bridge
Proceeding downstream keep well over to the left hand bank so as to get a straight run through the largest left hand arch.

Mooring available apply Castle Farm Cottage. Guest House at Castle Farm, ☎ (01832) 226200.

Perio Lock
At Fotheringhay, just downstream, earth mound remains of castle which was site of execution of Mary Queen of Scots. Inn/restaurant, public telephone. Good access for canoes at the road bridge on left bank. There is an EA water point upstream of Fotheringhay Bridge.

Bluebell Fisher
☎ 01832 2260

Warmington
Grange

Upstream
keep right

Bluebell
Lakes

Perio
Mill

Weir

TANSOR
No PH or shops

PERIO
LOCK

FB

Boat
Ho.

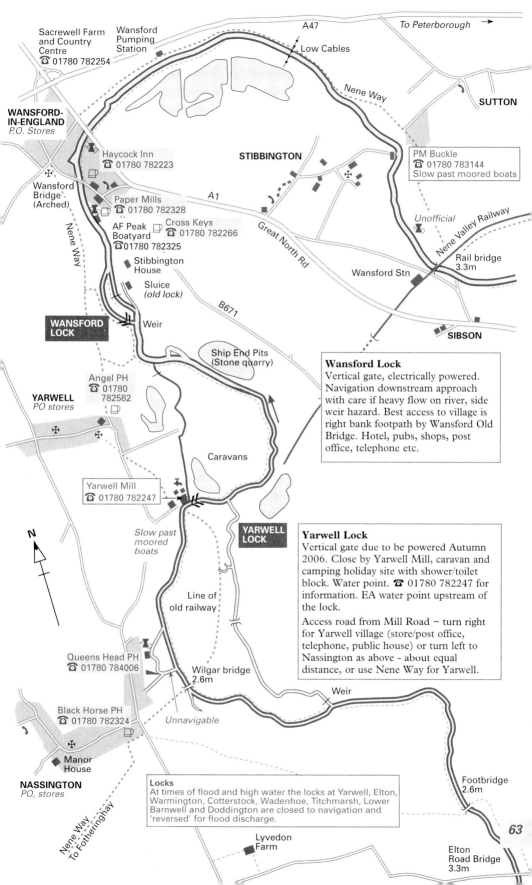

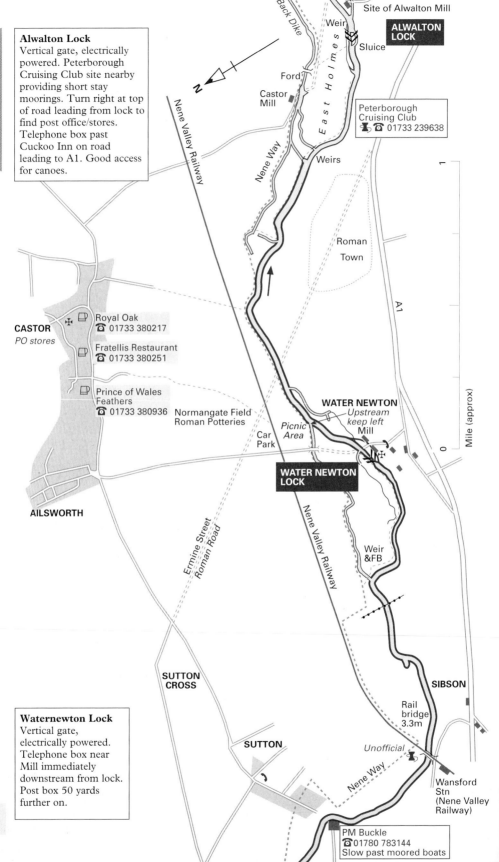

Alwalton Lock
Vertical gate, electrically powered. Peterborough Cruising Club site nearby providing short stay moorings. Turn right at top of road leading from lock to find post office/stores. Telephone box past Cuckoo Inn on road leading to A1. Good access for canoes.

Back Dike

Site of Alwalton Mill

Weir

ALWALTON LOCK

Sluice

Ford

Castor Mill

East Holmes

Peterborough Cruising Club
☎ 01733 239638

Nene Valley Railway

Nene Way

Weirs

Roman Town

A1

CASTOR
PO stores

Royal Oak
☎ 01733 380217

Fratellis Restaurant
☎ 01733 380251

Prince of Wales Feathers
☎ 01733 380936

Normangate Field Roman Potteries

AILSWORTH

Car Park

Picnic Area

WATER NEWTON
Upstream keep left
Mill

WATER NEWTON LOCK

Ermine Street Roman Road

Nene Valley Railway

Weir & FB

Mile (approx)

1

0

SUTTON CROSS

SIBSON

Rail bridge 3.3m

SUTTON

Unofficial

Nene Way

Wansford Stn (Nene Valley Railway)

PM Buckle
☎ 01780 783144
Slow past moored boats

Waternewton Lock
Vertical gate, electrically powered. Telephone box near Mill immediately downstream from lock. Post box 50 yards further on.

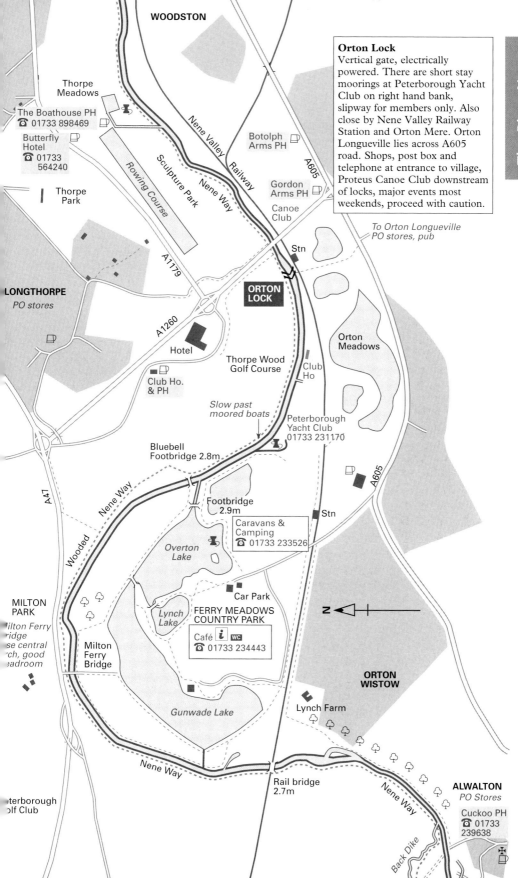

WOODSTON

Thorpe
Meadows

The Boathouse PH
☎ 01733 898469

Butterfly
Hotel
☎ 01733
564240

Thorpe
Park

LONGTHORPE
PO stores

Nene Valley Railway

Sculpture Park

Rowing Course

Nene Way

A1179

A1260

Hotel

Club Ho.
& PH

Botolph
Arms PH

A605

Gordon
Arms PH

Canoe
Club

Stn

**ORTON
LOCK**

Thorpe Wood
Golf Course

Club
Ho

*Slow past
moored boats*

Bluebell
Footbridge 2.8m

Nene Way

Wooded

A47

Footbridge
2.9m

Peterborough
Yacht Club
01733 231170

Caravans &
Camping
☎ 01733 233526

Orton
Meadows

*To Orton Longueville
PO stores, pub*

Stn

Orton Lock
Vertical gate, electrically
powered. There are short stay
moorings at Peterborough Yacht
Club on right hand bank,
slipway for members only. Also
close by Nene Valley Railway
Station and Orton Mere. Orton
Longueville lies across A605
road. Shops, post box and
telephone at entrance to village,
Proteus Canoe Club downstream
of locks, major events most
weekends, proceed with caution.

The River Nene

**MILTON
PARK**

Milton Ferry
Bridge
use central
arch, good
headroom

Milton
Ferry
Bridge

*Overton
Lake*

*Lynch
Lake*

Car Park

**FERRY MEADOWS
COUNTRY PARK**

Café *i* WC
☎ 01733 234443

Gunwade Lake

Nene Way

N

**ORTON
WISTOW**

Lynch Farm

Rail bridge
2.7m

Nene Way

Peterborough
Golf Club

ALWALTON
PO Stores

Cuckoo PH
☎ 01733
239638

Back Dike

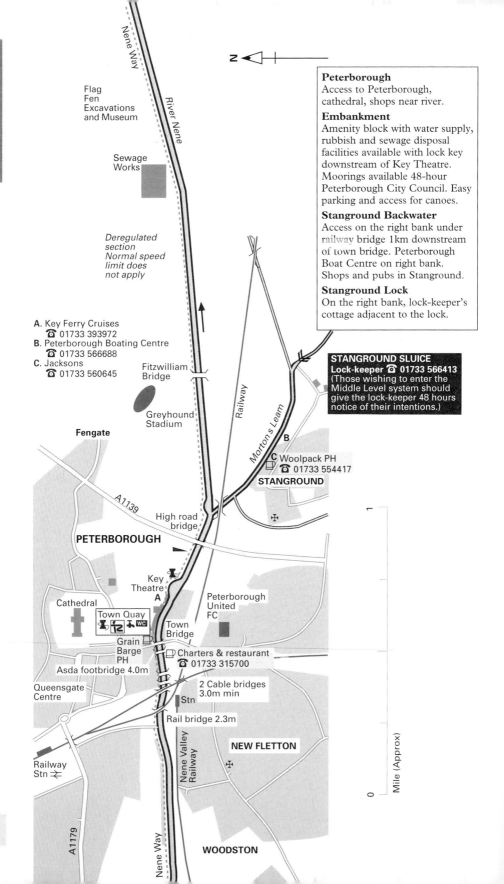

Flag Fen Excavations and Museum

Sewage Works

Deregulated section Normal speed limit does not apply

Nene Way

River Nene

N

Peterborough
Access to Peterborough, cathedral, shops near river.

Embankment
Amenity block with water supply, rubbish and sewage disposal facilities available with lock key downstream of Key Theatre. Moorings available 48-hour Peterborough City Council. Easy parking and access for canoes.

Stanground Backwater
Access on the right bank under railway bridge 1km downstream of town bridge. Peterborough Boat Centre on right bank. Shops and pubs in Stanground.

Stanground Lock
On the right bank, lock-keeper's cottage adjacent to the lock.

STANGROUND SLUICE
Lock-keeper ☎ 01733 566413
(Those wishing to enter the Middle Level system should give the lock-keeper 48 hours notice of their intentions.)

A. Key Ferry Cruises
 ☎ 01733 393972
B. Peterborough Boating Centre
 ☎ 01733 566688
C. Jacksons
 ☎ 01733 560645

Fitzwilliam Bridge

Greyhound Stadium

Fengate

Railway

Morton's Leam

B
C Woolpack PH
 ☎ 01733 554417
STANGROUND

A1139

High road bridge

PETERBOROUGH

Key Theatre
A

Cathedral

Peterborough United FC

Town Quay

Grain Barge PH

Town Bridge

Charters & restaurant
☎ 01733 315700

Asda footbridge 4.0m

Queensgate Centre

Stn

2 Cable bridges 3.0m min

Rail bridge 2.3m

Nene Valley Railway

NEW FLETTON

Railway Stn

Mile (Approx)

1

0

A1179

Nene Way

WOODSTON

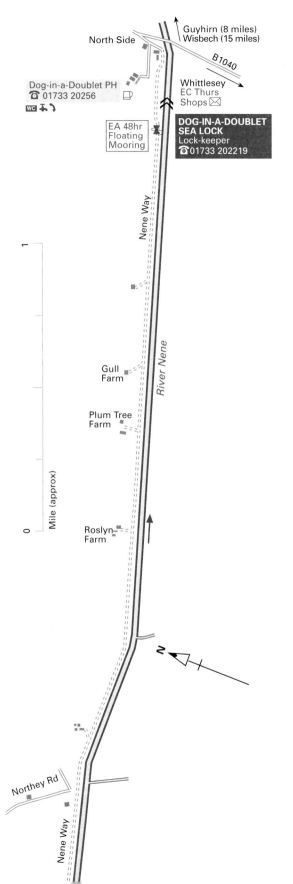

North Side

Guyhirn (8 miles)
Wisbech (15 miles)

B1040

Dog-in-a-Doublet PH
☎ 01733 20256
WC

Whittlesey
EC Thurs
Shops

EA 48hr
Floating
Mooring

**DOG-IN-A-DOUBLET
SEA LOCK**
Lock-keeper
☎01733 202219

Nene Way

River Nene

Gull
Farm

Plum Tree
Farm

Mile (approx)

1

0

Roslyn
Farm

N

Northey Rd

Nene Way

INDEX

Note: Page numbers in **bold** refer to maps